T0383521

To my family: without you, no house is ever a home.

To the people of the Béarn, and our neighbours in the
Pays Basque: *Merci, mercés, eskerrik asko*. Thank you
for your wisdom and for sharing this precious part of France.

HOW TO
FRENCH
COUNTRY

SARA SILM

CONTENTS

PREFACE: THE WAY HOME

'Monhor qu'ey lo mi vilatge au bèc du terrér renomat'
Montfort is my village on top of a renowned hill

From a *chansonette* in the Béarnaise dialect, composed in the early 20th century
by local songwriter Ernest Barrère.

THERE'S MAGIC IN THESE FOOTHILLS. A kind of colour sorcery cast with an invisible wand that renders everything in its wake pastel-smudged. With soft strokes of gentle watercolour hue, ends and beginnings blend into one, instantly erasing life's sharp edges and easing you into the safe, slow rhythm of country life.

Mornings here always begin with two sacred yet simple rituals: a mug of coffee in the peaceful silence of a slumbering household, and an early morning walk with the dogs along the old road that hugs the ridge above the river flats of the Gave d'Oloron. It leads through a dense forest of oak and chestnut, so damp and deeply green that its autumnal transformation never fails to evoke the same sense of childlike wonder that followed the slow turn of a kaleidoscope – colourful jewels of foliage, golden topaz, amber and garnet, gracefully falling into perfect patterns, as if by accident.

As daylight casts its spell over the darkened valley, it reveals powder-blue skies laced with clouds blushed pink and lavender like fairy floss at a fair; other mornings sombre and grey, storm-bruised with purple and steely blue as rain rolls in from the west. Beyond the road, there's an ever-changing patchwork of fields: wheat, alternating blue-green and silver as the wind weaves ribbons across the hillsides; swathes of buttery yellow sunflowers sandwiched between the rich chocolate voids of tilled soil. There are polka-dot pastures dotted with creamy Blonde d'Aquitaine cows lazily chewing their cud, and carpets of wild apple mint that pave your way with a crisp Granny Smith–green scent. And to accompany it all, the tinkle of sheep and cow bells, a bucolic sonata for the chorus of birdsong that ushers in the new day. These are the Béarnaise hills I call home.

———————

There's always been something magnetic about the simplicity of a rural existence, but in the wake of a global pandemic our need for nurturing is more profound than ever. Suddenly the thrilling buzz of city life has been replaced by a deep sense of vulnerability and isolation. The mass exodus from rural towns to cities that came with industrialisation at the turn of one century has ironically led to a yearning for the reverse at the beginning of another. The concept of urban abundance and the allure of unfettered choice have been replaced by images of long queues, endless rows of empty shelves and panic buying. When lockdowns temporarily eased, city dwellers around the world immediately flocked to the countryside for their holidays, leaving metropolitan centres largely abandoned. Suddenly, country real estate agents were busier than ever; city apartments swapped for farmhouses, with gardens to grow vegetables and fields to walk about freely … without a mask. If we didn't see a global pandemic coming, it's clear we still remembered the deep sense of comfort a simpler life could bring. For the first time in our living history, we've been forced to *stop*, punctuating the curly question of how we ever managed to complicate life with so much that didn't matter and, more to the point, that we have now proven we can live without.

Now more than ever, the dream of a slower lifestyle brings with it the ability to exercise some control over a world that has suddenly become unpredictable – and is likely to remain like that if we don't significantly alter our course. The pandemic was just part of a bigger ecological problem that has given us a moment for pause. Clearly country life is not the only solution, but its considered, seasonal focus reveals the secrets and wisdom of the past, which up to this point had increasingly been discounted as parochial. Since the Second World War, we've been bombarded with advertising 'solutions' to problems we simply don't have, all with the goal of selling us things we clearly don't need. Rather than making life easier, our world of plenty has eroded our confidence and our innate connection to the seasons – and with them, our direct access to food autonomy. Instant gratification has replaced seasonal traditions that were always led by the thrill of anticipation. We've become accustomed to the infinite and unattainable quest for more, when what we really need is less.

So, to that end, this book is a way home … to the way things were. To the violet bloom of a plum, just plucked from the tree; to the smell of a slow-cooked casserole when you open the front door on a cold night; to that soft, sinking feeling of melting into an armchair by a crackling fire and being handed a glass of local wine. It's a way of bringing a little bit of French country to your home, no matter where you live: an opportunity to paint away life's grey unknown with the reassuring colours of a French country landscape; to climb high into the Pyrénées with tales of adventure; to escape and meander along country lanes; to discover uniquely Béarnaise materials that might one day inform a renovation or inspire a future trip. In essence, it's a reflection on a simpler way of life, in a largely undiscovered region of France that has clung fast to its traditions, providing a gentler recipe for living and for refocusing on all that we hold dear.

PART ONE

PROVENANCE

THE ROAD TO *LE BÉARN*

SOME PEOPLE EMBARK UPON A NEW chapter in life with a grand plan. It certainly didn't happen that way for us. In fact, it was more like one of those old jokes that begin with 'three guys walk into a bar: one Aussie, one Irishman and a Pom' – only in our case, the bar was Irish, my husband and I were the Aussies, our friend was English and we were all eating curry at Mad Murphy's at the base of the Trans-Ili Alatau mountain range in downtown Almaty, Kazakhstan. My husband was working on a project there, our three children were all in boarding school in the UK and, after years of expat life in rented apartments, we were yearning for a home to call our own – albeit, at this stage, a holiday home. Life was complicated. We belonged nowhere. My husband was flying around Central Asia and Europe, I was bouncing backwards and forwards between a rented cottage in the English countryside near the children's school and our apartment in Almaty, and the only given in our lives was the constant, ever-pervading question that presents itself to every homeless globetrotter: 'chicken or beef?' Something had to change.

'Why don't you look around the Béarn?' said our English friend, Blair, who'd bought a holiday house in the region years prior. 'You'd love it! In winter you can be out the front door, clicked into your bindings and skiing in less than an hour. In summer you can be at the beach surfing in the same amount of time. In between, you can hike, river raft, and generally just have a jolly good time drinking French wine in the sun.' Jason and I looked at one another in that resigned, unspoken way couples do, finished our Baltika beer and went back to the apartment to book flights for a four-day whirlwind tour.

When we arrived in the Nouvelle-Aquitaine region of south-west France, we were shown through an endless array of empty nests: some ostrich-sized, some more on the sparrow side, but all, as the French like to say, *dans son jus* – or as we say in English, a renovator's delight. My brief to the real estate agents was only to show me old homes that hadn't been renovated; I didn't want to spend one centime on someone else's 'improvements' when what that really meant was costly demolition. We visited the grand

---

A GLIMPSE OF THE VALLÉE D'ASPE ON THE GR10 ROUTE FROM LA PIERRE SAINT-MARTIN TO LESCUN, WHICH CROSSES FRANCE FROM THE ATLANTIC TO THE MEDITERRANEAN.

chateaus that wowed us on the internet, only to find that their vast gardens had been subdivided and they were surrounded by housing estates, a water-slide park or, in one very special case, a pungent sewage works. Some agents took me at my word and showed me treasures so original we needed to stand under an umbrella in the sitting room. One thing was for sure though, Blair wasn't lying when he said we'd love the Béarn – we'd fallen head over heels in love with it. The only problem was, we hadn't quite found our little piece of it.

The night before we were due to fly back to Almaty, I scoured the internet until that little bit of something found me. The listing simply said, 'Béarnaise country house with sweeping views and a large garden bordered by a stream and small orchard'. I called the agent the next morning, and serendipity stepped in. 'I've just had a cancellation,' she said, 'but I have viewings all day. I could give you twenty minutes if you think that would be enough.' 'We'll be there within the hour,' I said, finishing my café au lait and madly shoving clothes into our suitcases.

It sounds so clichéd – and I'm loath to describe it this way – but it's true, sometimes houses really do find you. And when you step inside them, you really do know, instantly, that this is where you'll fill the coming chapters of your life. That day, I think I'd only just reached the foot of the staircase when I discovered this for myself. The house had been empty for more than two decades. There were sheets thrown over the furniture, and as the agent opened the shutters, thousands of tiny specks of twinkling dust floated around me like feathery white flakes in a snowdome. It really was the stuff of fairytales. Although others might have just smelt the damp, and seen the dirt and the years of abandonment entangled in thorny brambles and ribbons of peeling paint, I saw a home, our home – and in just a few weeks, it and everything underneath those dust sheets was ours.

ANNABELLE, GATHERING WILD CARROT FLOWERS (OR QUEEN ANNE'S LACE)
IN THE VILLAGE OF ARAUJUZON, NEAR MONTFORT.

CHÂTEAU MONTFORT

Although the house is known locally as *le Château*, it's actually a *maison de maître*, or 'master's house'. These homes were built between the 18th and 19th centuries by the bourgeoisie or local gentry, who usually made their living from landholdings and agricultural rents. A typical *maison de maître* has a symmetrical facade with a central door and shuttered sash-style windows on either side. Our home has been given the far grander title of '*château*' simply by virtue of the somewhat ostentatious addition of two towers, and because it is the largest house in a very modest village of just 184 inhabitants. In spite of this exaggerated title, what attracted me was its understated charm. It's essentially a village house, set on a little 'no-through' lane … but it reveals itself slowly. It's not boastful or proud and its rooms aren't large – in fact, they're remarkably modest – and from the very first day I entered its darkened hallways, the walls hinted at a history of happier days.

Adjacent to the house is the *conciergerie* (a three-bedroom cottage), and a little further down the lane is the farm manager's cottage. Once part of the estate surrounding the *maison de maître*, these two buildings were sold off many years before we purchased it; in fact, all the land on the ridge once belonged to *le Château*, including a small vineyard, now long gone. The house was built by a General Duplantier in the mid-19th century, and when eventually there was no Duplantier heir left to inherit, it was sold to Monsieur and Madame Personnaz. The couple had notable ties to both Basque heritage and the Belgian royal family: Madame Personnaz was the sister-in-law of King Leopold III of Belgium, via his second marriage to her sister, Mary Lilian Baels, Princess of Réthy.

Sadly, the home's history of notable proprietors came to an abrupt end the day two unknown and unimportant Australians moved in with their three children. But it seemed happy to have our company nonetheless – and, as laughter and love returned, it shook off its long years of silence and embraced each of us as one of its own. Floorboards once more began to creak, the shutters let out a contented yawn as they were opened each morning, and the light from the chandelier above the dining room table blinked on and off excitedly as the children charged around the bedroom above, playing hide and seek. We were home.

THE HOUSE, THROUGH A SEA OF LUSH PASTURE AND BUTTERCUPS.
A ROW OF ANCIENT PLANE TREES TO ITS REAR.

OVERLEAF: EARLY SPRING IN THE GARDEN. LIME-GREEN BRACTS OF EUPHORBIA,
MARSHMALLOW-PINK AND WHITE MAGNOLIA AND PURE WHITE PLUM BLOSSOM HUG THE
HOUSE WITH THE PROMISE OF LONGER DAYS AND NEW LIFE.

OPENING DOORS AND UNLOCKING SECRETS

The day we took possession of the house, the agent gave me an enormous set of old keys. They were so big and so heavy that just carrying the front door key with me on a quick outing to buy bread required a large market basket, mostly for the key. Inside the house there were yet more keys. Every door had a key with a little handwritten label – even the armoires and chests of drawers each had a key.

The day I first unlocked the front door, I was on my own. I'd flown in for two weeks to get the renovations underway, because living in the house at this stage was more like camping. I wandered around the empty house like Goldilocks, removing dust sheets and sitting on chairs, turning keys, opening doors, unlocking secrets.

When I opened the huge armoire in the central hallway on the first floor, I found regimental piles of starched maids' aprons, monogrammed sets of fine linen sheets, heavy cotton damask bedcovers, and piles of antique fabrics and trims. In the library on the ground floor, I carefully blew away the dust from ancient leather-bound books and turned their fragile pages. There were books on art and history – and vast collections of poetry and French literature. In addition to numerous bibles and rosary beads, I found photo albums dating back to 1898, containing time-faded images of grand tours around the most elegant homes of Europe; pictures of Edwardian ladies dressed in fine gowns and elaborate hats having garden parties and sipping tea, and men in white suits with walking canes and panama hats. There was a suitcase full of letters from aristocrats and diplomats, and Christmas cards featuring watercolour scenes of sleds in the snow with some remaining scant traces of ancient glitter. In the attic I found framed photos of grand old ladies, as well as portraits of once-cherished babies. In the drawers of the office desk, I uncovered monogrammed stationery, old letter openers and blank postcards of Spanish dancers with little glued-on fabric skirts. There were boxes of paperclips, old pots of ink, nibbed pens and balls of string. In the kitchen, beneath a soft fuzzy layer of mould, were old Limoges plates, Spode platters and terracotta casserole pots. It was like lifting the lid on a box of incomplete puzzle pieces; like a silent movie that abruptly runs off the spool partway through. There were so many clues, but no answers, and still to this day the identity of these people remains a mystery.

It was April, and I'd given myself the mission of making the house liveable by Christmas. I'd fly in for two weeks and out for two weeks, project managing while I was away and working on the restoration alongside the team of French artisans when I was there. We began with a total overhaul of the plumbing and electrics, repairs to collapsed ceilings and floors, and a completely new roof – as well as the addition of three new bathrooms and, for good measure, a new kitchen and a butler's pantry. I'm never one to shy away from a challenge, but this was one of my most ambitious yet.

A SET OF THE ORIGINAL HOUSE KEYS.

35

On that first day, I visited all the bedrooms until I found one on the first floor with a key that simply said, in old-fashioned scrolled French handwriting, *Maman*. I took two sheets and an old woollen blanket from the armoire and went to a coin-slot laundry in the local supermarket carpark. Upon returning home, I pegged the clean sheets and blanket onto a worn piece of rope between two trees in the garden, to dry in the sun. I swept and dusted and aired and scrubbed and disinfected until the kitchen was free of mould and the bedroom was clean. And then, just like Goldilocks, I settled down for my first night in an old bed that was impeccably clean and – surprisingly – not too soft, not too hard, but just right. The neighbours all thought I was completely mad. 'Aren't you scared … all alone in that big house … in that old bed and without any back doors on the house?' they said. The truth was, I wasn't. I've never been one for watching scary movies, and my early years spent watching *Scooby Doo* proved without a doubt that there was always a logical explanation when it came to imagined ghosts or things that go bump in the night. What's more, I wasn't exactly on my own.

There was Julie: an old oil painting (which has a tag identifying the subject by name) of a beautiful lady in a gown of fine white satin and a shawl of plush red velvet. She was originally hanging in the darkened sitting room, so I moved her to take up pride of place in the entrance hallway. Her hair falls in ringlets from two loose bunches above each ear and she has those Mona Lisa eyes that follow you no matter where you stand in a room. From the moment Julie came out of the dark she's watched my every move. She's the first to set eyes on me in the morning and the last to watch me climb the stairs at night. Her expression never changes. She looks at me nonchalantly over her left shoulder, not smiling, not frowning, just demurely observing. In those early days, as I came down from painting the bedrooms on the first floor, she'd look at me somewhat smugly, as if to say, 'By the way, you missed a bit on the architrave.' Other days her eyes would be fixed with a more quizzical stare as if to say, 'That casserole smelt quite good last night. Did you use a splash of that Bordeaux in the cellar?' Much of the time now she just looks at me with the kind of matriarchal expression that says, 'Really? Are you really going to run into town again wearing that horrific paint-splattered boilersuit … *again*, Sara?' Mostly, she's non-judgemental, and over the years we've struck up a loyal friendship – although the children, who *have* watched one too many horror movies, think she's 'completely creepy' and refuse to make eye contact with her.

THE PORTRAIT OF JULIE, LOOKING JUST AS SHE ALWAYS DOES – DEMURE, EYES FIXED ON WHOEVER DARES TO LOOK AT HER.

A TOUR OF THE HOUSE

I felt that at the start of the book it would be useful for me to take you on a quick tour of the main house. The details of these rooms will become very familiar to you as we move into the more practical half of the book, where I discuss the various design elements involved in creating the interiors.

Among its various outbuildings, the house also has a barn, '*La Grange aux Tourterelles*'. The barn's transformation offers a perfect case study of 'how to French country' – and so it has its very own section further along in the book.

The entry hall

The entry hall, besides having had a new lick of paint, remains just as we found it. The old encaustic tiles and oak staircase were given a good clean – using warm water and a good slosh of Marius Fabre savon noir soap – and the space softened with a made-to-measure natural jute hall rug edged with cotton. The oil painting of 'Julie' that we found in the sitting room of the house was repositioned on the wall above an old oak chest, which was in exactly the same position when we moved in. Our hall table was brought over from Australia (it's made with reclaimed Australian hardwood), although it's since been moved to the barn and replaced with a red-and-grey marble-topped antique table that goes beautifully with the wallpaper. The walls are painted in Farrow & Ball Estate Emulsion, colour Mole's Breath, and the trims are Farrow & Ball Estate Eggshell in Cornforth White and Purbeck Stone. The Little Greene wallpaper is High Street Rouge, from the London Wallpapers III collection.

THE DOOR AT THE END OF THE ENTRY HALL LEADS TO THE WALLED GARDEN.
THE HALL IS HOME TO A CROQUET AND BOULES SET, A COLLECTION OF VINTAGE BOTTLES
AND A CHAMPAGNE CRATE FULL OF OLD JARS FOR DISPLAYING SEASONAL FLOWERS
FROM THE GARDEN.

The lounge room

The walls in the lounge room have been painted with Farrow & Ball Casein Distemper in Mole's Breath. The beautifully soft, matt finish of casein distemper is nuanced in the way only natural paints can be. Its velvety finish is intended to keep the lamp-lit room feeling very intimate and cosy. The kilim floor rug was purchased at Moscow's Izmailovsky Market during our time living in Russia. It brings with it not only wonderful memories but also colour, pattern and a touch of the exotic, adding soulful character to what could ordinarily feel like quite a formal room.

The ground floor bedroom

This room is a teen-cave. It's rarely exposed to daylight and its occupant can generally only ever be reached by text message or Béarnaise sheep bell. Just to annoy the macho inhabitant, the walls have been painted in Little Greene Intelligent Matt Emulsion in Light Peachblossom. The floors are covered with sustainably made woven vinyl, by Bolon.

The ground floor bathroom

Originally a bathroom with a vast storage cupboard, the dimensions of this room have remained unchanged. Demolishing the cupboard made room for a big claw-foot bath and separate shower; we retained the original enamel pedestal vanity and old taps. The bathroom's walls were simply painted in Farrow & Ball Modern Emulsion, colour String, and lined with bevel-edged white subway tiles. The floors are tumbled travertine marble from Cupastone. There is an adjoining wall between the ground floor bathroom and the study, allowing it to be used as a powder room when there are guests, as well as an ensuite.

THE LOUNGE ROOM. THE ANTIQUE KNOLE SOFA WAS REUPHOLSTERED IN A DUSTY MAUVE-PINK VELVET BY ATELIER MENDIKOA USING TIME-HONOURED TRADITIONAL TECHNIQUES. THE LAMPS WERE BOUGHT IN LOCAL *BROCANTES* AND THE SILK IKAT CUSHIONS WHILE ON HOLIDAY IN ISTANBUL.

ABOVE: A MARBLE-TOPPED TABLE I FOUND AT ONE OF MY FAVOURITE *BROCANTES*, PAINTED IN A MIXTURE OF LEFTOVER AUTENTICO CHALK PAINTS I MIXED MYSELF. A BOUQUET OF SPRING FLOWERS SITS IN AN OLD CONFIT POT – THESE MAKE THE MOST WONDERFUL WIDE-MOUTHED VASES!

OPPOSITE: THE VIEW FROM THE ENTRY HALL TO THE LIBRARY STUDY. THE OLD ENCAUSTIC FLOOR TILES LAY HIDDEN BENEATH A LAYER OF STUBBORN GLUE AND MOULDY CARPET. ONE BY ONE THEY WERE PAINSTAKINGLY RELEASED FROM THEIR TOMB TO ONCE AGAIN MEET THE FOOTFALLS OF A BUSY FAMILY.

The library study

This room was originally the study. The stately old oak library shelves were once housed in the internal verandah library. We carefully moved them and adjusted them to fit the walls of the study, where their collection of ancient leather-bound books now resides. This is the darkest room of the house, only receiving light in the late afternoon. Rather than paint it a very light colour, I decided to exaggerate the low light and paint it in Farrow & Ball's deep, inky Hague Blue, adding task lighting with desk lamps, a floor lamp and a pendant light. Hague Blue is a handsome hue that's very reminiscent of an old-fashioned men's smoking room – which is fitting, because it's where my husband works when he's not travelling. The beautiful painting of the Greek goddess Athena above the fireplace came with the house, as did the old desk.

The dining room

This room features a beautiful carved fireplace in an exotic wood that, I'm told, was brought back from Indochina by General Duplantier before he built the house. It was carved by local Béarnaise artisans. The oak dining table was bought at a local *brocante* for €50. I painted the legs in Autentico Vintage chalk-based paint, colour Flannel Grey, and applied Autentico's dark brown wax finish to highlight the carved details. The timber tabletop was sanded and waxed with natural beeswax polish. I have collected the antique bentwood chairs over many years, and had them all re-caned by a wonderful artisan at my local market. The marble-topped sideboard was an antique market find. I think I paid just €40 for it. It wasn't in the greatest condition, so I employed Autentico's Vintage chalk-based paint again (this time in Foggy Venice), using the dark brown wax to emphasise the beautiful carved detailing.

THE DINING ROOM. SPRING HYACINTHS IN AN OLD DOUGH-PROVING TROUGH SIT ATOP THE DINING TABLE, SURROUNDED BY AN ASSORTMENT OF THONET BENTWOOD CHAIRS. THE MANTELPIECE HOUSES A BRIC-A-BRAC COLLECTION OF BIRDS' NESTS, CERAMICS, ONE OF MY OWN SCULPTURES (A PREGNANT ME WITH BABY HUGO ON MY HIP) AND A WHITE MARBLE BUST THAT WAS IN THE HOUSE WHEN WE BOUGHT IT.

The kitchen

Sometimes when you're designing a kitchen in an existing house, you just have to work with the footprint available. Our heavy stone walls are approximately 50 centimetres thick; not only that, but we live opposite a 13th-century heritage-listed church – so any alterations to the original facade would have been both complicated and extremely costly. Instead, I worked with the galley-style kitchen we inherited, converting it into a butler's pantry, and joined the verandah library and scullery to make one long main kitchen, with an adjoining snug. The small kitchen table was in the original kitchen.

I opted for a neutral colour palette here, sticking to just one tone in the Farrow & Ball series, Ammonite, for both the base cabinets and the wall cabinets. The wall tiles are all simple bevel-edged white subway tiles and the floor tiles are tumbled travertine marble from Cupastone. I designed the raw tulipwood timber cabinetry to fit the space. They were manufactured by a British company called Handmade Kitchens of Christchurch and shipped, pre-assembled, to France, where they were handpainted in situ. The duck-egg blue electric AGA was purchased secondhand in the UK and shipped to France – Aggie AGA, as she is known, is more than a mere cooker, she's a genuine member of the family. Our sink is made from one huge, solid piece of stone; it's shallow, so I use it for its original intended purpose – for washing vegetables from the garden, arranging flowers and day-to-day handwashing. The plumbing is hidden with a simple handspun raw linen skirt, which is hung on a plastic-coated wire with two small brass eyelets fastened to a wall hook on either end.

THE LINEN FABRIC USED FOR THIS TABLECLOTH WAS FOUND AT BOUCHARA, A HOMEWARES CHAIN IN FRANCE THAT ALSO SELLS WELL-PRICED, GOOD QUALITY LINEN BY THE METRE – SIMPLY HEM IT AND *VOILA*. SORELY UNDER-UTILISED, TABLECLOTHS TURN FUNCTIONAL FURNITURE INTO A SURFACE FOR PATTERN AND RUSTIC TEXTURE. BUY SEVERAL PATTERNS SO YOU CAN ROTATE THEM ON A REGULAR BASIS.

LEFT: THE OLD STONE SINK, USED MAINLY FOR WASHING VEGETABLES HARVESTED FROM THE *POTAGER*, ARRANGING VASES OF FRESHLY CUT FLOWERS, WASHING HANDS AND, AFTERWARDS, SPLASHING FACES – HOT AND IN NEED OF REFRESHMENT AFTER GARDENING – WITH THE SOOTHING SCENT OF ROSEWATER (KEPT IN A BLUE GLASS BOTTLE NEXT TO THE SOAP).

CENTRE: AN OLD AUSTRALIAN HARDWOOD TOOL BENCH, HOME TO A COLLECTION OF KITCHEN UTENSILS. ON THE WALL ARE A COLLECTION OF ANTIQUE FRENCH CHEESE BOARDS.

RIGHT: THE INDISPENSABLE, ALMOST INVISIBLE, KITCHEN FLY SCREEN INVENTED BY OUR BRILLIANT CARPENTER, DÉDÉ. THANKS TO ITS RETRACTABLE BLIND-LIKE MECHANISM, THE KITCHEN WINDOWS CAN BE LEFT OPEN, ALLOWING THE HEAVENLY SCENT OF STAR JASMINE TO GENTLY BLOW IN ON THE BREEZE WHILE LEAVING THE FLIES OUTSIDE, WHERE THEY BELONG.

THE BELOVED HEART OF THE HOUSE, THE DUCK-EGG BLUE AGA. ABOVE THE STONE SINK
TO THE REAR HANGS A BRANCH OF BAY (EXCELLENT FOR DETERRING FLIES AND SCENTING
THE AIR WITH ITS FRESH, SPICY FRAGRANCE) AND A STRING OF PIMENT D'ESPELETTE.

JASON, GRILLING VEGETABLES ON THE ORIGINAL HEARTH IN THE SNUG.

The snug

The snug, or small sitting room, was the original kitchen when the house was built. It has a separate maid's entrance via the back corner of the room (though that's now clearly meant for me) and access to the cellar, where we store wine and preserves. The huge hearth is an extension of the kitchen in the cooler months. It's a cosy space we all love; close enough to the action in the main kitchen for me to feel part of the conversation if I'm cooking, but far enough away to keep the family snuggled up on the sofa and removed from the fray. We regularly use the fireplace in winter to bake jacket potatoes in the coals, chargrill steaks and vegetables, and roast chestnuts and marshmallows – so the big hearth is still feeding the family, just as it has done for over 200 years. The original sofa and armchairs that were here when we bought the house are still in this room; I simply made washable slipcovers for them. The exotic caramel-coloured cowhide blends beautifully with the creamy tumbled travertine tiles that also run through the kitchen. There are no overhead lights in this area – I've intentionally kept it very cosy; just lamp light and the golden glow of the fire.

The butler's pantry

The butler's pantry was the kitchen when we moved in. The cabinetry that was in place was excellent-quality solid oak, but some of the base cabinets had begun to rot. I salvaged what I could, keeping the wall cabinets and the base cabinets below the big windows, and designed cabinetry with simple Shaker-style doors for a new section along the long side of the room. To subtly differentiate this room from the new kitchen, I worked from the main neutral colour palette for the house, grounding the base cabinets with a deep shade of brown-grey (Farrow & Ball Mole's Breath), then working up in tone to Farrow & Ball Ammonite, a subtle calming grey, and, finally, making it a little cosier by darkening the walls slightly with Farrow & Ball Cornforth White. The big window that looks out over the front field is painted Farrow & Ball Strong White. This lightening gradient of tone gives the room an air of space and height. I used the same white bevel-edged subway tiles that are in all the bathrooms. If you have a number of rooms to tile, buying in bulk is often very cost-effective, particularly if you're working within a tight neutral palette where a simple white tile will suffice for multiple areas. The benchtops here are the same as the main kitchen, Silestone quartz composite, colour Lagoon. I placed task

THE BUTLER'S PANTRY WINDOW, HOME TO AN EVER-CHANGING ARRAY OF FRESH PRODUCE FROM LOCAL MARKETS AND THE *POTAGER*, AS WELL AS CAKES AND, IN THIS CASE, FUDGY HOMEMADE BROWNIES.

lighting under the wall cabinets, and from the ceiling I hung a vintage-style pendant light with a simple fluted glass shade. The taps are Perrin & Rowe Ionian Bridge Style in polished chrome, with a retractable spray nozzle for rinsing plates. The encaustic floor tiles I designed myself, using the same colour blue as the AGA in the kitchen and colours from the neutral grey-and-white palette.

The tall tower bedroom, sunroom and bathroom

The tall tower bedroom, once belonging to 'Papa', was in a bad way when we bought the house. There was a hole in the roof above it and water had crept in, causing the entire ceiling to collapse. Because it was a large room and we needed to construct a new ceiling, we decided to lower it slightly and add wool insulation to help conserve the heat in winter. The walls that are not papered feature a collection of framed watercolours, photos and etchings that I found in the attic, as well as some old framed menus from my great-grandmother's travels by ocean liner around Europe. The jute rug was made to measure for the room, and the beautiful antique French *corbeille* (or *capitonné*) style bed was bought from an antique store.

The small tower bedroom, sunroom and bathroom

This room was originally much smaller, but we consolidated the staircase to the attic, removing the return to make it a single flight, and gained space to enlarge the bedroom behind it and create a dressing area below. The sunroom that adjoins it was once a large, long room with the towers located at each end. We decided it would be nicer for each of the two bedrooms on this side to have its own private sitting area, with an ensuite bathroom created within each tower. Of all the bedrooms, this one required the most work. We enlarged the small window that was there, creating a lovely view out over the walled garden, and consolidated the stairs and demolished the internal dividing brick wall. Once the debris was removed, a new plaster wall was built, with a door added to separate the dressing area gained from the underside of the attic staircase.

A LAZY SUNDAY MORNING IN THE SHORT TOWER BEDROOM, WINDOWS THROWN OPEN, THE DELICATE PERFUME OF CYCLAMEN ON THE BREEZE.

LEFT: MORNING LIGHT IN THE TALL TOWER BEDROOM.

CENTRE: THE ENTRANCE TO THE TALL TOWER BEDROOM. A SERIES OF FRAMED OCEAN LINER MENUS FROM MY GREAT-GRANDMOTHER'S WORLD CRUISE HANG ON THE WALL, WHICH IS PAINTED IN FARROW & BALL LIGHT BLUE. DOOR, SKIRTING BOARDS AND ARCHITRAVES ARE IN FARROW & BALL AMMONITE.

RIGHT: THE SHORT TOWER BATHROOM. DRAPED OVER THE BATH IS A BASQUE BAÏNAS
TOWEL FROM LARTIGUE 1910. THEY'RE A KIND OF BEACH TOWEL THAT'S QUITE UNIQUE
TO THIS AREA, BUT I PREFER TO USE THEM AS BATH TOWELS AS THEY DRY MUCH FASTER
THAN REGULAR FLUFFY TOWELS.

The blue bedroom

I love the colour of this room – Little Greene Intelligent Matt Emulsion in Juniper Ash – it's the colour of the sky here in the Béarn just before a summer thunderstorm. The beds were purchased from Selency, a great antiques website, while the bedside table, armoire and desk were bargains from *vide-greniers* (empty attics) – the French version of a car boot sale, only much more exciting!

The toile bedroom

Once the room of '*Maman*', this bedroom sits opposite that of '*Papa*'. It is very simply painted in Little Greene Intelligent Matt Emulsion, colour Slaked Lime. I found the beautiful antique floor rug in a *brocante* and brought the long antique pine chest of drawers over from Australia and then painted it in Scandinavian Blue Autentico Vintage chalk-based paint. The original bed was reupholstered in a simple natural linen with an aged bronze-stud trim.

The toile bathroom

This is the original bathroom. I adore a bit of wallpaper in the bathroom, especially toile, because to me it always tells a story – which is lovely when you take the time to let your imagination run free as you relax in the bath. Here I used Little Greene Stag Toile in Juniper. The design – which comes from a piece of 19th-century English linen – is washable, meaning it's suited to bathrooms. One thing I would caution against is having wallpaper too close to shower areas; ideally, these should be tiled. If you're using wallpaper in a bathroom, ensure that the wallpaper is not in any direct contact with water on a regular basis and always install a ventilation fan to reduce steam and condensation.

The green bedroom

This bedroom, which is narrow and long, has a beautiful view out across the front field. Inspired by the view over pastures, I painted the walls in a soft green by Little Greene called Salix. The antique iron king-single beds are both from Australia; one is the bed I slept in as a child. I kept the original curtains in

THE GREEN BEDROOM IS ONE OF THE QUIETEST AND MOST PEACEFUL ROOMS IN THE HOUSE, NO DOUBT DUE TO ITS CALMING GREEN WALLS IN LITTLE GREENE SALIX.

LEFT: THE BLUE BEDROOM ALWAYS FEELS COSY, WITH ITS CHEERFUL
WOODBLOCK-PRINTED COTTON QUILTS AND CUSHIONS BY CAÏ FAHREL.

CENTRE: THE TOILE BEDROOM. AN ANTIQUE PINE CHEST PAINTED IN AUTENTICO SCANDINAVIAN
BLUE OFFERS A CALM PLACE FOR THE EYE TO REST AMID THE SURROUNDING PATTERNS OF THE
VINTAGE RUG AND GALLERY OF ANTIQUE BOTANICAL PRINTS BY PIERRE-JOSEPH REDOUTÉ.

RIGHT: THE TOILE BATHROOM. WITH THE EXCEPTION OF THE WALLPAPER, EVERYTHING IN
THIS ROOM, THE ORIGINAL BATHROOM OF THE HOUSE, IS EXACTLY AS IT WAS WHEN WE MOVED IN.

the room – they're a romantic old French Les Indiennes pattern – and tied-in organic hemp bed linen by the French manufacturer Couleur Chanvre, in coordinating plain colours derived from the pattern. The antique floor rug I found locally at a charity shop, and the chest of drawers was originally in the house. (My advice for decorating is always to use what you have. If something is meaningful to you, if it's well made, functional and well designed, but a little shabby – reinvent it. The less demand there is for modern mass-produced furniture, the better off the planet will be.) The green room is one of our guest rooms. One thing I love to do in children's rooms and guest rooms is to put a few fresh drops of organic French lavender oil onto little lavender bags and place them under the pillows when I make the beds. Fresh flowers from the garden and a bottle of pure local Ogeu mineral water – from a spring in the Pyrénées – are two other welcoming essentials for the bedside.

The attic

The attic comprises an entire floor with the same footprint as the rest of the house, but it's yet to be renovated. The top of the tower on this floor was once the maid's bedroom, with scant traces of the original wallpaper still clinging to parts of the wall. The remainder of the attic is a receptacle for accumulated junk – ours and that of each previous owner of the house. The views from any of its seven windows are quite spectacular, especially the views of the Pyrénées.

The garden

The garden is made up of four main areas. The *potager* is the place where I grow seasonal vegetables, herbs, apples and soft fruit. The larger, park-style garden features perennial beds for cut flowers; we also have a fire pit here, perfect for teenage parties and associated overnight camping – when they're not being held down at the river. The kitchen terrace and pool area adjoins the kitchen and is essentially an extension of the house in the warmer months, even up until Christmas. This is where we cook most meals in summer, on our custom-made barbecue, which has a wall-mounted metal rack for burning logs. We use fig wood, bay branches and grapevine prunings, called *sarments* (available from our local Jurançon vineyards), to impart a delicious, subtle flavour to grilled meat and fish.

THE ATTIC, OTHERWISE KNOWN AS THE 'WAITING PLACE', IN WHICH TREASURES FOUND OR SOMEHOW ALREADY THERE COME TO SIT FOR A BIT, AWAITING RESTORATION, PAINTING, FIXING OR INSPIRATION.

When building any beds for my garden I use the 'no-dig' method, which basically involves laying a thick base of paper and cardboard on the ground's surface, and then building up lasagna-like layers of compostable organic materials, such as straw and manure, along with more paper and cardboard. Not only does this method build the soil, conserve moisture and subdue weeds but it also ensures that all your household paper waste is recycled. Cardboard packaging, boxes, wastepaper … they're all used on the garden. To this I add well-rotted manure and straw from my neighbour's barn – his cows' bedding.

The animals

We have a motley crew of chickens: five rescued from a battery farm (who are known as The Supremes) and various others purchased from local markets, including our rooster, Richard, who was being eyed up in a rather 'culinary' way.

I always have a scrap bucket on the kitchen bench, which is emptied into a larger bucket outside the kitchen door. All our kitchen scraps – excluding meat – go into this bucket, and every day the contents are tipped into the chicken run. The chickens then eat the scraps and leave anything they don't want, which I add to the compost heap. Keeping the compost close to the chicken run makes it easy to add the manure from the chickens' shelter on a weekly basis; their droppings are too strong to put straight onto the garden.

Our chicken house is in the old outdoor laundry. I've laid a solid floor over the top of the original wash troughs and placed recycled ladders above for perching. Once a week it's just a simple matter of scraping off the manure from the surface into a bucket, using an old cement trowel, and then adding it to the compost to break down. I scatter wood ash from the fire to absorb moisture inside the hen house; I also scatter the ash inside the nesting boxes to deter red mites and absorb any odours, before adding fresh straw each week.

We keep Nubian-cross milking goats to help control the once-rampant bamboo that has been used to stabilise the nearby riverbank beyond the stone ha-ha (also known as a *saut-de-loup*, or 'wolf jump'). This sunken supporting structure separates the formal gardens from the bottom field, where magnificent oak, walnut and spruce trees take centre stage amid a field of native pasture.

CLOCKWISE FROM TOP LEFT: THE GOAT SHED. BUILT, I'M PROUD TO SAY, BY AN ALL-GIRL CREW: ANNABELLE, OUR FRIEND ESTER AND MYSELF. WE USED RECYCLED PALLETS AND TREATED PINE CLADDING. FIVE YEARS ON, IT'S STILL STANDING! ● THREE LOCAL DONKEYS, LIKE A ROW OF UNSTACKED MATRYOSHKA DOLLS. ● ESTHER THE NUBIAN-CROSS GOAT, UP CLOSE. WHEN THE PHOTOGRAPHER IS YOUR MOTHER, THE LENS GETS IN THE WAY OF KISSES. ● TOBY WITH ONE OF OUR NEIGHBOURS' DONKEYS THAT REGULARLY COME TO STAY AND HELP OUT WITH 'MOWING THE GRASS' IN THE BOTTOM FIELD.

PART TWO

BRINGING FRANCE HOME

FRENCH COUNTRY COLOUR

IT WASN'T UNTIL I MOVED TO THE BÉARN that I saw colour in a truly northern light. As an Australian, I learned to style and shoot houses in the harsh southern sun; this often saw me out of bed before the dawn to catch the colours before (as we say in photography) they 'blew out' and became a paler, less interesting version of themselves. Likewise, when I was choosing colours for houses, they often needed to be just a touch higher in chroma (pigment content) to stand up to the elements and retain their true hues.

Here in the Béarn, it's a different story. The light is diffused. Even on a summer's day, there's always a slightly mauve-grey tinge to it. The palette of both landscape and buildings is a gentle combination of greyed-off blues, greens, pinks and earthy ochres, which retain their colour – but never too much of it – in the face of the elements. They are always in harmony, throughout all the seasons and in any kind of weather.

Béarnaise neutrals, for the most part, derive from the ubiquitous natural building materials: creamy white limestone and river stone; sandy lime-render that is tinted ochre, salmon-pink or taupe; pointy-pitched slate and terracotta roofs – featuring the typical Béarnaise 'witch's hat brim'. The grey-patinated exposed oak beams and floorboards of the local houses marry beautifully with the stone walls typical of the Béarn, forming the perfect palette for soft whites and subtle greys.

What provides the main colour canvas in Béarnaise architecture is the use of painted shutters and doors. The colours used will be slightly different from those in the surrounding areas of Les Landes and the Midi-Pyrénées. But they are *vastly* different from those right on its doorstep in the Pays Basque, where walls are rendered a stark white and shutters are painted in one of only four colours: Basque brown, Basque red, Basque green or Basque blue. There are no other choices; nor would any proud Basque family ever consider them.

A TYPICAL BÉARNAISE VILLAGE FARMHOUSE, DRAPED IN A BUNTING OF WISTERIA.

THE MEDIEVAL STREETS IN THE
STUNNING VILLAGE OF SAUVETERRE-
DE-BÉARN (ALSO SEEN ON PAGE 88).

OPPOSITE: A HOUSE WITHIN THE
FORTIFIED MEDIEVAL WALLS OF
NAVARRENX, WHICH WAS AWARDED
THE PRESTIGIOUS TITLE OF BEING
AMONG *LES PLUS BEAUX VILLAGES
DE FRANCE* (THE MOST BEAUTIFUL
VILLAGES IN FRANCE).

A FOREIGNERS' GUIDE TO FRENCH SHUTTERS

Shutters are among the most charming architectural elements of the French country home, but they serve a far greater purpose than simple adornment. One of the biggest mistakes that foreigners make when they come to France is to wake up on a sunny summer's morning, fling open the shutters and windows, and go about their day. This is *not* what shutters are there for. If you look at a French country house on a hot summer's day, you'll see the shutters are always almost completely closed, left ajar just a crack. This is because the house is aired when the morning air is cool, after which the shutters are closed to block out the sun and the heat of the day. In combination with the thick stone walls of the typical French country house, the result is astounding. We have no need for airconditioning in summer; our house is always cool. In winter, we retain the warmth in the bedrooms by keeping the shutters closed in the morning and airing rooms when the temperature rises later in the day.

DEFINING YOUR FRENCH COUNTRY STYLE

The general perception of a French country home and lifestyle can be somewhat generic. But just as French cuisine is proudly regional, so too are the daily rhythms of life, the seasonal colours of the landscape, the architecture, the dialects, local traditions and decor. A French country home in Provence will look very different from one here in the Béarn. And by the same token, although Château Montfort is steeped in local history and built with regional materials, my home is as much a reflection of my life as a globe-trotting foreigner as my neighbours' home is of their life and that of the five generations who preceded them there. There's always a balance between the inhabitant and the provenance of the building; and so, for this reason, the results of my renovations by no means represent a classic example of a Béarnaise country home.

They are, however, informed and guided by the colours of the local landscape, the artisanal materials that are unique to this region and by the seasonal, slow lifestyle I've come to adopt as my own. This is where authenticity comes in. Just as it would be considered absurd and downright blasphemous for a farmer from the Béarn to build a Basque-style house on their plot of land, it would also be disingenuous of me to suggest that you – despite clearly being a lover of all things French country – should reproduce everything I suggest in your own home. Your home is *your* home, and for it to feel authentic there needs to be a balance between what *inspires* you and what *defines* you. This book is merely a guide, a way of taking you by the hand and leading you down the lanes of the beautiful, and in many respects undiscovered, region of France that I now call home. A way of showing you how I arrived at my version of French country, in the hope that it might inspire yours.

So how do you find what's 'you' while still evoking an undeniably French country aesthetic? When I set out to design an interior, my first step is to take a pen and paper and imagine how I would want to feel in that as-yet imaginary room. I list the smells, textures, colours, sounds and light, and the provenance – the personal associations and memories – that this ideal interior elicits for me. This is my *feel board*. I would strongly encourage you to create your own. If you're able to identify the emotive elements of an interior – those that resonate with you, those that meaningfully engage your senses and give tangible form to the way you want to feel in a room – the result will always be aesthetically matched, cohesive and authentically you.

AN OLD INDUSTRIAL TABLE TOPPED WITH SENTIMENTAL TREASURES: A SOVIET CAVIAR TIN, A PAIR OF BALLET SHOES FROM MOSCOW'S BOLSHOI THEATRE AND MY FAVOURITE CIRE TRUDON CANDLES AND ROOM SCENT. THE LAMP'S BASE IS AN OLD SPIRIT STILL, PAIRED WITH A MADE-TO-MEASURE SHADE BY ABAT-JOUR ETC. IN ORTHEZ, USING FRINGING FROM FRINGE MARKET AND FABRIC FROM CLARKE & CLARKE (SISSINGHURST DESIGN, COLOUR MIDNIGHT/SPICE).

CAPTURING THE COLOURS OF THE BÉARN

As a colour enthusiast, I well remember my first months in the Béarn, walking around local villages with my head constantly cranking upwards, then forwards, then up again, as I collected photos of shutters and doors in their hundreds. I saw shutters in my sleep; subtle shades of blue so close to one another … yet just different enough to make me revisit those houses again and again. What was it that made them so special, I wondered; there couldn't have been that many shades available fifty or sixty years ago when they were painted. And then I realised: this was baked-in patina. I began to notice that blue-painted shutters and doors on the south-facing sides of buildings were slightly more sun-faded compared with their north-facing cousins; these were more weather-beaten in appearance, after decades of being battered by storms blown inland from the Atlantic. Some paint colours were so old – and flaking away so badly – that only a single precious chip remained, clinging to the timber. It was at this stage that I decided to start collecting samples and convert each one into an international paint code that could be authentically reproduced to create an exact version of the original.

Like any collector, I wanted to keep a record, an archive, safely stored away. But I also did it because there's one question I'm always asked by people who've visited France and left with a burning desire to bring a little bit of it back to their home: 'How do I find the perfect French blue?' (Followed by: 'Where would I find that beautiful green door colour?' And the questions keep coming …)

There are certainly plenty of commercial colours that fulfil this brief to perfection, and I've arranged a series of colour choices for you in the pages that follow. But what you can't find in a paint catalogue are the paint codes I've created myself. I've collected these colours in the same way a mad botanist walks the fields and mountains collecting plants and seeds. Some of them will never be seen again, because their years of patina will have disintegrated into tiny fragments by the time this book is published. Some will have weathered away forever. Other codes represent just a small part – the most beautiful part – of a painted shutter or door, which I felt had weathered to absolute perfection. What's more, these colours are Béarnaise (except in the case of Saint-Jean-de-Luz, which is Basque) – and can only be found in this book.

The colours have been categorised into the towns in which they were found and paired with their Natural Colour System (NCS) colour code, to create a kind of colour by numbers, if you will. So, if you see a colour that would be perfect for your front door (or, for that matter, for your bedroom wall), simply take the code to a paint-supply store with the facilities for mixing international paint colours and, with the shake of a tin, it will be yours.

NCS codes are also used by the manufacturers of a wide range of design products and decorative materials such as tiles, flooring, doors, cabinets, kitchens, furniture, textiles and wallpapers – which means that you can have joinery, tile glazes and much more custom-coloured in the Béarnaise palette.

AN OUTLANDISH PINK HOLLYHOCK ADORNS A MEDIEVAL STREET CORNER IN SALLIES-DE-BÉARN, WITH JUST A CRACK IN THE PAVEMENT AS ITS FOOTHOLD.

NAVARRENX

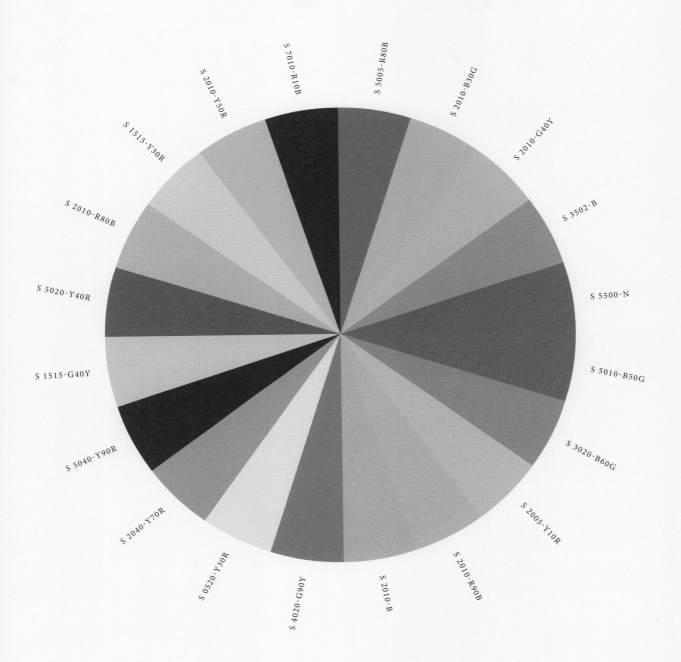

S 7010-R10B
S 5005-R80B
S 2010-Y50R
S 2010-B30G
S 1515-Y30R
S 2010-G40Y
S 2010-R80B
S 3502-B
S 5020-Y40R
S 5500-N
S 1515-G40Y
S 5010-B50G
S 5040-Y90R
S 3020-B60G
S 2040-Y70R
S 2005-Y10R
S 0520-Y30R
S 2010-R90B
S 0520-G90Y
S 2010-B

ORTHEZ

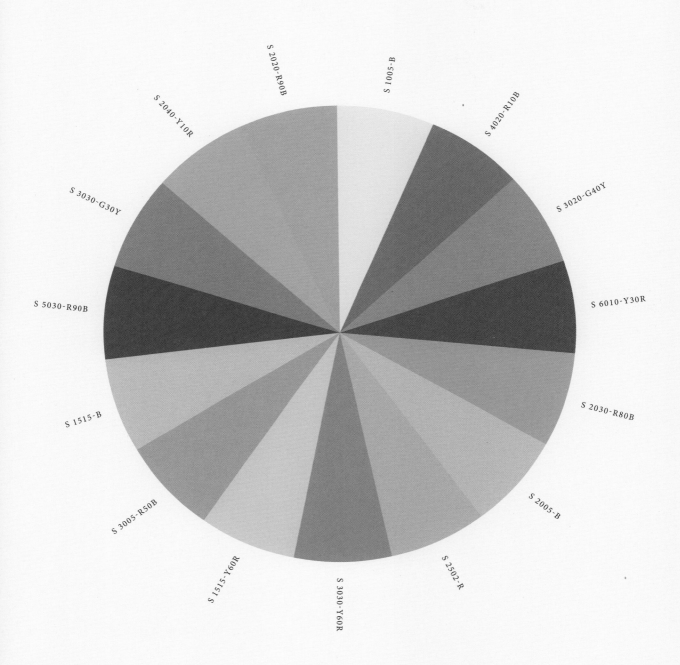

S 1005-B

S 4020-R10B

S 3020-G40Y

S 6010-Y30R

S 2030-R80B

S 2005-B

S 2502-R

S 3030-Y60R

S 1515-Y60R

S 3005-R50B

S 1515-B

S 5030-R90B

S 3030-G30Y

S 2040-Y10R

S 2020-R90B

OLORON-SAINTE-MARIE

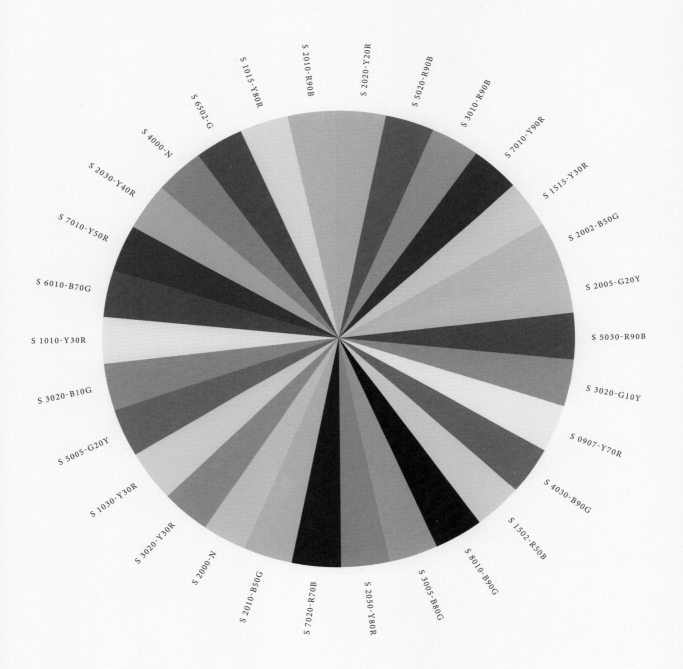

PAU

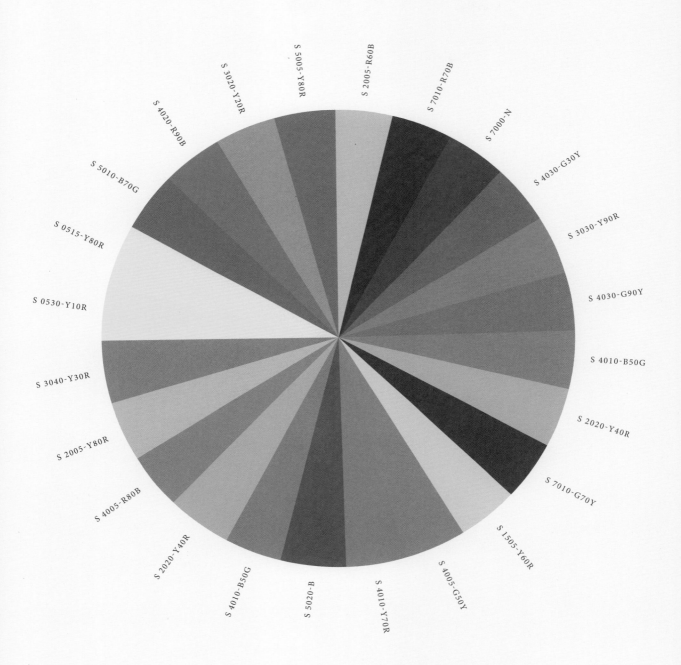

S 2005-R60B
S 5005-Y80R
S 3020-Y20R
S 4020-R90B
S 5010-B70G
S 0515-Y80R
S 0530-Y10R
S 3040-Y30R
S 2005-Y80R
S 4005-R80B
S 2020-Y40R
S 4010-B50G
S 5020-B
S 4010-Y70R
S 4005-G50Y
S 1505-Y60R
S 7010-G70Y
S 2020-Y40R
S 4010-B50G
S 2005-R60B
S 7010-R70B
S 7000-N
S 4030-G30Y
S 3030-Y90R
S 4030-G90Y
S 4010-B50G
S 2020-Y40R

SAINT-JEAN-DE-LUZ

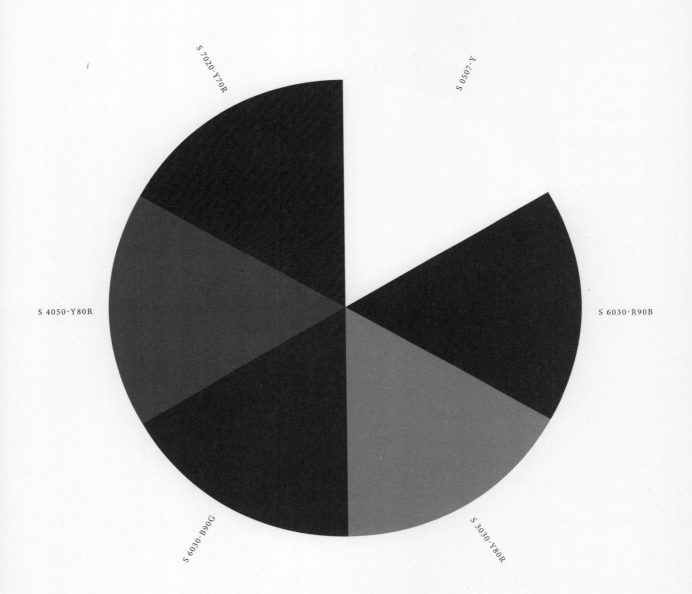

S 7020-Y70R

S 0507-Y

S 4050-Y80R

S 6030-R90B

S 6030-B90G

S 3030-Y80R

SAUVETERRE-DE-BÉARN

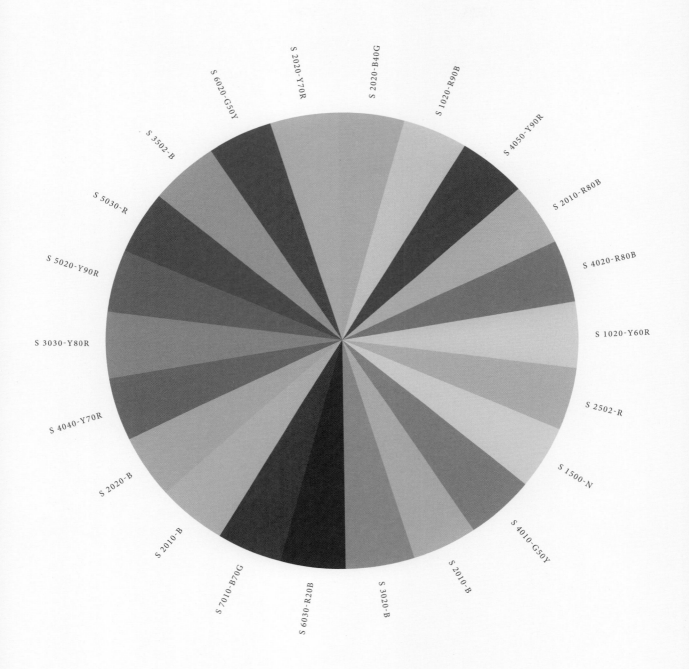

COMMERCIAL PAINT
COLOUR PALETTES

The following colour palettes are entirely based on the seasonal hues of the Béarnaise landscape and its surrounds. They're a selection of commercial paint colours I've matched to things I've come across in everyday life; everything from fishing nets on a day trip to the coastal town of Saint-Jean-de-Luz to the soft green fuzz of freshly picked young almonds. If you are not able to source some of these paint brands in your country, try matching your selected colour or colours to the closest hue in an available brand. If in doubt, ask your paint supplier for advice; there are often more colour options in what's called the Master Palette, which professionals generally use.

There are absolutely no rules about where a colour should be used in your house. You could easily paint your kitchen cabinets in one of these shades of pink or you could play it safe and stick to a neutral. The beauty of these colour palettes is that they're a little family, tonally harmonious and equally as happy in one another's company as they are with a basic grey or shade of white from the neutral palette. I've deliberately kept them tonally and chromatically close, which gives you the reassurance that they will always blend beautifully throughout the house, without jarring or clashing with one another.

STRIPED BEACH TENTS ON *LA GRANDE PLAGE*, SAINT-JEAN-DE-LUZ.

Beach tents, macarons and *crème glacée*

The muted pinks, greens, blues, mauve and taupe in this palette are *so* easy in one another's company that you could use them in pairs (i.e. on walls and woodwork) or even introduce a third or fourth colour from this palette into the room (for example, one colour on the skirting boards and windows, one on the walls, another for a contrasting piece of furniture).

1. BENJAMIN MOORE, PUTNAM IVORY **2.** LITTLE GREENE, RUBINE ASHES **3.** RESSOURCE, BEIGE FOIN S108
4. RESSOURCE, MORTLAKE BLUE HC78 **5.** LITTLE GREENE, CELESTIAL BLUE **6.** RESSOURCE, PALE MEDICI BLUE HC57
7. RESSOURCE, GRIS MAUVE S26B **8.** LITTLE GREENE, BLUSH **9.** FARROW & BALL, SETTING PLASTER
10. LITTLE GREENE, BONE CHINA BLUE **11.** RESSOURCE, PALE VERDURE GREEN HC62 **12.** LITTLE GREENE, JAMES
13. BENJAMIN MOORE, GEORGETOWN PINK BEIGE **14.** BENJAMIN MOORE, YELLOW BRICK ROAD **15.** ARGILE, TERRE GRIS

I've included yellow in the palette to show how chroma (intensity of colour saturation) can draw one's eye. All the colours in this palette – except for the yellow – are tonally fairly similar; they all sit at roughly the same level of lightness/darkness, and their hue is more or less the same level of chroma. The yellow, however, has a higher chroma level. In the terminology of colour science, yellow has a more dominant wavelength than the other colours in the spectrum, providing more stimulation for the light receptors in our eyes. These receptors transmit messages to the brain, enabling it to differentiate one colour from another. Notice the way your eye is immediately drawn to the yellow shell – but when it comes to the other colours, it happily skims from one to the other. The tip here is that the higher the chroma of a colour, the more of a diva it becomes.

If you're naturally drawn to bright colours, but you also love the more muted French country palette, that's fine. Just try to use the high-chroma hues proportionately, as a feature. For example, you could paint a rustic kitchen stool or bench in Yellow Brick Road by Benjamin Moore and have it sitting against a mudroom wall painted in Little Greene Blush, or any of the other colours here for that matter. High-chroma colours are not necessarily part of the traditional French country palette – but I firmly believe that you have to be true to yourself. Bright colours, bright yellow in particular, are joyous and uplifting. If you love a colour, find a way to be authentic and let your personality shine through. It could be something as subtle as a huge vase of bright yellow buttercups collected on a morning walk in the countryside, or a vintage yellow milk jug … or perhaps a huge yellow sunhat on a coat rack.

I have a bright yellow lamp in the snug and a bright yellow ceramic crock to store my *échalotes* in the main kitchen; they're small elements that give me that happy pop of yellow I love without overwhelming the overall palette.

REDUCING THE CHROMA OF A COLOUR

There are two ways to reduce the chroma – the intensity or saturation – of a colour: you can either mix the colour with its complementary hue (that is, the colour that sits directly opposite on a standard colour wheel), or you can add a similar tone (depth or shade) of grey.

By blending complementary colours you get a beautiful range of muted colours (which I refer to as the 'landscape palette'). For example, in the case of mixing orange with its complementary colour blue, you get gorgeous, sludgy olive greens, as well as terracottas, caramels and teals – all of which are everywhere in the local Béarnaise landscape. Having created these hues, you can reduce the chroma even further by adding greys of various tonal values.

This technical information shouldn't define your colour choices – these must be entirely guided by what makes you feel best – but it's interesting to know that colours aren't just made lighter or darker by adding white or black.

THE BRIGHT YELLOW SHUTTERS AT DOMAINE DE CABARROUY IN LASSEUBE, ONE OF THE MOST BEAUTIFUL VINEYARDS IN THE JURANÇON VALLEY.

WILDFLOWER-STREWN SPRING
PASTURE OVERLOOKING THE
BEAUTIFUL VALLEE D'ASPE.

Peaks, forests and streams

This colour palette comes from some of my favourite hikes in the Pyrénées: through the beautiful forests of the vallées d'Aspe and d'Ossau, along mountain streams with moss and lichen. And from hunting for mushrooms: head-down, inhaling that earthy aroma of decaying leaves and forest floor.

1. LITTLE GREENE, TEA WITH FLORENCE **2.** ARGILE, BLEU BURLINGTON **3.** LITTLE GREENE, EDITH'S EYE
4. LITTLE GREENE, PUTTI **5.** ARGILE, BLEU CENDRÉ **6.** LITTLE GREENE, LIVID **7.** AUTENTICO, DENIM
8. AUTENTICO, GRIS **9.** AUTENTICO, POETIC **10.** FARROW & BALL, HAGUE BLUE **11.** FARROW & BALL, LIGHT BLUE

THE LOUNGE ROOM, SEEN FROM THE ENTRANCE HALLWAY. THE YELLOW TAPESTRY CHAIR WAS FOUND AT A LOCAL ANTIQUES STORE. THE CHEST TO ITS LEFT WAS IN THE EXACT SAME SPOT WHEN WE BOUGHT THE HOUSE.

Adventure, kilims and vintage Les Indiennes

This palette was inspired by my collection of kilim rugs and exotic vintage textiles. There's a whiff of cigar smoke in this palette, a drop of cognac and the sultry rhythm of jazz. If your personal feel board has any elements of adventure, the exotic, romance, literature or perhaps a touch of sassy bravado, then you might find something here.

1. LITTLE GREENE, LIGHT BRONZE GREEN **2.** AUTENTICO, PIGEON GREY **3.** RESSOURCE, CLAIRE DE LUNE HC35
4. RESSOURCE, DEEP CELADON GREEN HC41 **5.** LITTLE GREENE, BAKED CHERRY **6.** AUTENTICO, FRENCH GREY
7. AUTENTICO, MAUVE-FAUX **8.** AUTENTICO, MORNING MAUVE **9.** LITTLE GREENE, GARDEN
10. BENJAMIN MOORE, PHILIPSBURG BLUE **11.** LITTLE GREENE, YELLOW-PINK **12.** LITTLE GREENE, CITRINE
13. LITTLE GREENE, ASHES OF ROSE **14.** BENJAMIN MOORE, ASHLEY GREY **15.** LITTLE GREENE, JUNIPER ASH
16. AUTENTICO, LAVENDER **17.** LITTLE GREENE, CARMINE **18.** AUTENTICO, INDIAN SAND

THE COOL SPRING SNOWMELT FEEDS
THE GAVE D'ASPE, WHICH SNAKES
ITS WAY THROUGH THE OLD TOWN OF
OLORON-SAINTE-MARIE IN A SWATHE
OF MOODY BLUES AND MOSSY
GREENS. NOT FAR DOWNSTREAM,
THE GAVE D'ASPE CONVERGES WITH
THE GAVE D'OSSAU TO FORM THE
BEAUTIFUL GAVE D'OLORON, WHICH
RUNS PAST MONTFORT.

An homage to the Gave d'Oloron

This palette is inspired by our river, the Gave d'Oloron. It runs from the snow-capped mountain peaks of the Pyrénées and straight past our house. These colours come from its depths and its sandy shores, from its rapids caught amid raging crests of foam, and from the feeling of gently running your toes across slimy, smooth stones on a hot summer's day.

1. FARROW & BALL, OVAL ROOM BLUE **2.** ARGILE, ARDOISE VERTE **3.** BENJAMIN MOORE, STONINGTON GRAY
4. LITTLE GREENE, FRENCH GREY **5.** BENJAMIN MOORE, SHERWOOD GREEN **6.** BENJAMIN MOORE, SOUTHFIELD GREEN
7. BENJAMIN MOORE, JAMESTOWN BLUE **8.** FARROW & BALL, LICHEN **9.** BENJAMIN MOORE, PALLADIAN BLUE
10. FARROW & BALL, VERT DE TERRE **11.** BENJAMIN MOORE, WOODLAWN BLUE **12.** FARROW & BALL, SKYLIGHT
13. LITTLE GREENE, SALIX **14.** ARGILE, VERTE DE VÉRONE

101

THE BUTLER'S PANTRY
WINDOW IN SPRING.

A handy palette of neutrals

Neutrals are the bread and butter of the paint pantry. Shown here are the neutrals used throughout the main house. They are all tonal variations of the same neutral base; that is to say, from Mole's Breath upwards they become tonally lighter with the addition of white. If you use a family of neutrals that are related, that is from the same base, then your neutrals will flow seamlessly, no matter which tonal variation you choose.

NOTE: ALL PAINTS BY FARROW & BALL.
1. MOLE'S BREATH **2.** AMMONITE **3.** STRONG WHITE
4. PURBECK STONE **5.** CORNFORTH WHITE

THE PRACTICALITIES OF PAINT

IF YOU'RE NEW TO DIY PAINTING OR ARE keen to try something different from a standard wall emulsion, fear not: it's only paint. Repeat after me: *it's only paint*. If for some reason you don't like the result, just paint over it. But before you do, my advice would be to wait a few days. For many of us, change – even when we want it – can sometimes come as a shock, so let it settle. See how the colour changes throughout the day and try to imagine how it might look if other elements in the room were a different colour. If it's not immediately to your liking, it might be as simple as a change of cushion covers to complement the new wall colour or painted piece of furniture; or a different set of curtains … or no curtains at all. Paint is just one element in a room. Take your time, take everything in, and let it mellow.

When I worked with interior design clients, it was always paint colours that caused the greatest angst. Each and every time, my soothing words were always the same. *It's only paint.* Let's walk through this together – it's not nearly as scary as you might imagine. And for those of you who throw yourselves at a tin of paint with gay abandon, let's go!

FURNITURE PAINT

I often use chalk-based paints on my furniture. The most common term for this family of paints is 'Chalk Paint', which is in fact the name copyrighted by Annie Sloan in the 1990s, when she developed her beautiful range of paints specifically designed to be used on furniture without the need for priming or sanding. Since then, a range of other chalk-based furniture paints have come on to the market. I primarily use two European brands, Autentico (Dutch) and Liberon (French). Both are typical of this type of paint – matt with a soft, almost velvety, finish, thanks to the base of calcium carbonate (limestone). There are many excellent paints available in this category, so explore what's available to you locally.

Calcium carbonate is also responsible for the beautiful, chalky patina of these paints. However, it leaves the surface porous (think of a stick of chalk in water), so it's important to seal the dried paint surface with a clear wax finish or matt varnish to provide protection from daily wear and tear, as well as greasy fingerprints. Just remember that a coat of clear wax or matt varnish will darken the colour slightly; when you choose a chalk-based paint colour based on a little brush-out from a sample pot, it's often a good idea to rub a little clear wax onto the swatch when it's dry. Of course, you don't have to seal the paint with wax if you don't want to, especially if the surface isn't going to be touched in the general course of its life – a roof beam, for example.

The joy of using this kind of paint is that it's fun and incredibly easy to apply. If I'm using a chalk-based paint, I rarely sand or apply a base coat to furniture. The only time I'd bother with either is if the furniture is particularly greasy or the timber has a sappy residue. Or if stain has been applied to the wood, which might bleed through the paint. If you're worried about this, simply refer to your chalk-based paint manufacturer's catalogue and apply their recommended stain-proof base coat.

Inevitably, painted furniture will show signs of wear with use, particularly on the edges of drawers and doors as well as any protruding carved detailing – but this is part of the charm of chalk-based paint. It's unapologetically relaxed and rustic, which lends itself perfectly to the French country aesthetic.

Another furniture paint I often use is milk paint, or casein paint, made with clay, milk-protein powder (casein), calcium carbonate, pigments and water. It's very similar to chalk-based paint, just slightly thinner in consistency and often sold in powder form that you mix with water. I use Liberon casein paints, which come pre-mixed in a ready-to-use formulation. What are the main differences between milk-based and chalk-based furniture paints? I've used both, a lot, and in my opinion milk-based paint tends to give a slightly more rustic finish, allowing imperfections and wood grain to show through a little more than chalk paint does. I used milk-based paint on the windows and skirting boards in one of the barn bedrooms and found its slightly thinner consistency on the brush easier to cut-in than chalk-based paint. But, apart from that, I find the depth of colour and flat finish of both chalk-based and milk-based paints equally appealing.

NEVER UNDERESTIMATE THE CHARM OF A KEY TASSEL. THEY CAN BE USED TO ADD A SUBTLE KISS OF COLOUR OR, AS IS THE CASE HERE, AN EARTHY TOUCH OF TEXTURE.

Painting kit

Both chalk- and milk-based furniture paints are water-based. I always clean my brushes with warm water and Marius Fabre liquid savon noir soap; a traditional and biodegradable French soap made from olive oil. The natural oils in the soap help to keep the paintbrush bristles supple. If for any reason you get water-based paint on clothing, simply massage a little liquid savon noir onto the paint stain, leave overnight and then wash. It does a great job!

I use a natural-bristled sash brush, bought from a local hardware store, for my furniture pieces. These brushes have a long, slim head with the bristles coming to a point, making them ideal for cutting-in to awkward areas, like corners and carved details. There's no reason you couldn't use a larger round or flat brush, or even a small roller if the piece is large (though I've never used one). It's really just down to personal preference and the amount of bristle patina you want on your piece – the bigger the brush, the more pronounced the brushstrokes. Keep in mind that it's not only the brushstrokes that create a patina; each piece of handpainted furniture will be slightly different based on the person applying the paint. The length and rhythm of the brushstroke application, and the size/shape of the brush, both combine to create a subtle personal signature. You don't need to buy the brush sold by your paint manufacturer – I purchase my natural-bristled brushes from the local supermarket or hardware store.

One piece of specialist equipment I *would* recommend, though, is a wax brush. This is a short, stumpy-handled brush that you can easily dab into pots of wax, making application even and easy on the wrist. I bought mine from Autentico years ago and simply keep it tightly wrapped in wax-proof paper when it's not in use. I reserve this brush for clear wax and use scraps of soft cloth for taking off any excess. When it comes to dark wax, though, I use the cheapest natural-bristle brushes I can find (craft paintbrushes from discount shops are good).

I also keep scraps of soft, lint-free cloth – such as old 100 per cent cotton sheets, singlets and T-shirts – on hand. I use these for rubbing-back areas of paint in order to create a worn-patina effect – best done fifteen to twenty minutes after you apply the paint. If you take off too much, you can simply paint over the rubbed-back area and try again, with a little less force. I also use cloths to rub off excess wax.

If you haven't already got one, I swear by a good old boilersuit for any DIY painting jobs. There's nothing more satisfying than wiping paint all over your clothes and parading around a hardware store looking like a real professional.

ANOTHER LIFE FOR SAMPLE POTS

If you have ordered chalk-based paint sample pots and only used a dab from each, save them for smaller projects. They're perfect for painting inexpensive or salvaged timber picture frames, and for small bric-a-brac finds such as old mirrors, lamp bases and storage boxes. IKEA's mini storage drawers, which are made out of natural wood, are ideal for painting in one of your feel board colours; use them for spice storage in the kitchen or for bits and bobs in the office.

One slightly off-piste thing I do is to mix sample pots of chalk-based paint to make my own colours. As long as you're mixing chalk-based paint from the same brand, nothing can really go wrong from a technical point of view. The only risk is that you'll mix a colour you don't like — and if that's the case, you can simply paint over it with another one. The single word of caution I'd offer is to make sure you use a uniform measure, like a measuring jug or measuring spoons, so you can record the quantities and reproduce the colour if ever you need it again. Add paint in small portions and test it as you go. It's like adding salt to food — once you've added too much (pigment) there's no going back! That said, what's a few sample pots? Experiment and have fun, that's what colour is all about.

CHALK-BASED FURNITURE PAINT COLOURS

The colours that follow are from the paint companies I have access to and enjoy working with. That said, there are many other reputable chalk-based paint suppliers to choose from. If you can't find these brands, have fun experimenting with those you do have access to. And remember, *it's only paint*.

SAVON NOIR AND SAVON DE MARSEILLE

Savon de Marseille and savon noir soaps are both plant-based, phosphate-free, 100 per cent natural and completely biodegradable. The production process for both is fairly similar: they are made the traditional way, in huge cauldrons, from a blend of vegetable oils (including olive oil), salt and a base product to turn the oils into soap.

Savon de Marseille has a soda base, which makes it an extremely gentle soap for washing the face, body and hair – it is often recommended by dermatologists for use on sensitive skin. Its component vegetable oils are olive oil or coconut oil, which are equally gentle. It is great for washing delicates in the laundry as well as for general household cleaning. Savon de Marseille is also a great deterrent for clothes moths: simply store a block of the soap with your linen or hang it in your wardrobe – the adult moths hate the smell of the oil, which deters them from laying eggs.

Savon noir uses a base of potassium, which makes it an excellent stain remover and multipurpose cleaner for cutting through grease; its component vegetable oils are flax oil and olive oil. Savon noir's usefulness doesn't stop at the front door. I use diluted savon noir on all my roses. Aphids hate it, as does powdery mildew. If you use this soap in the kitchen or for cleaning, save the water from the sink and mop buckets and use it on the garden; there is nothing in it that can harm plants – in fact, savon noir is certified for use on organic farms. It also makes an excellent dog wash and is used by organic dairy farmers to wash the udders of dairy cows, sheep and goats before milking.

Chalk-based neutrals

NOTE: ALL PAINTS BY AUTENTICO.
1. CEMENT **2.** BATH STONE **3.** AFTER RAIN **4.** COCOS
5. BRUT **6.** NEUTRAL **7.** ROMAN WHITE

THE VALLÉE DE BARÉTOUS. THE
RED-BROWN BRACKEN THAT GROWS
ON THESE HILLS IS TRADITIONALLY
HARVESTED AND USED AS AN
ALTERNATIVE TO HAY FOR BEDDING
IN BARNS AND TO THATCH THE ROOFS
OF PIG HUTS.

Coast and countryside

NOTE: ALL PAINTS BY LIBÉRON.
1. ARGILE **2.** BELLE ILE **3.** BORD DE SEINE (PLATE BENEATH IN RUBAN)
4. GRIS FLAMANT **5.** CELADON **6.** BRUME (PLATE BENEATH IN ORAGE)
7. EPI DE BLÉ (PLATE BENEATH IN VELOURS OCHER) **8.** CHAMPIGNON

LAC D'ARTOUSTE, VALLÉE D'OSSAU.

Foggy mornings and clear skies

NOTE: ALL PAINTS BY AUTENTICO.
1. MAUVE FAUX **2.** SEA MOSS **3.** PIGEON GREY **4.** SWEDISH BLUE
5. CASTLE GREY **6.** BARI **7.** WILDERNESS **8.** SURRY HILLS **9.** ICELAND

TOP LEFT TO BOTTOM RIGHT: FIRST COAT; WOOD PUTTY APPLIED TO WOOD-BORER HOLES; DARK WAX APPLIED TO CARVED DETAILS BEFORE EXCESS IS REMOVED; THE FINISHED PIECE.

How to paint a piece of furniture with chalk-based or milk-based paint

1. Remove any dust for maximum paint adhesion. If I'm painting a large piece of furniture, I vacuum it using a soft brush attachment and then give it a quick wipe with a damp cloth. If the piece feels greasy, dampen the cloth with hot, soapy water; this usually isn't necessary unless it's had a particularly grubby past life. Ensure the piece is completely dry before painting. I've never sanded a piece of furniture before applying chalk-based paint, but if there are any areas on the piece that are rough and jagged, do this now.

2. Apply a stain-block primer/undercoat from your chalk-based paint supplier if the piece has been treated with a wood stain. Occasionally tannins found in woods such as mahogany, oak, chestnut and pine can bleed through to the paint surface when they come into contact with moisture. This has only happened to me once, with white chalk-based paint. I rarely apply a primer.

3. Apply the chalk-based paint to your furniture. There's nothing neat or precise about the application; in fact, just the opposite. Simply whack it on with crisscross brushstrokes, ensuring you have an even application that's not too thick. Don't worry if the wood shows through this coat, you merely want the paint to bond to the surface. This stage should come with a panic alert. I've often painted the first coat onto large pieces of furniture and then stood back in horror thinking, 'What *have* I done?' It always looks like a spotty teenager after the first coat; so, take a deep breath and walk away for at least one to two hours while it dries, knowing all will be well after a nice cup of tea and a second coat.

4. If you return to discover that your vintage piece has some nasty pockmarks, these may be the work of wood borers. They often become apparent after the first coat of paint. Don't worry. Simply fill the holes with wood putty (I use a pre-mixed paste out of a tube) and allow to dry completely before giving the puttied areas a light sand and applying the second coat using the same crisscross brushstrokes. Allow to dry.

5. Apply the clear wax. I like to do this with the same long crisscross brushstrokes, preferably using a wax brush. If necessary, wipe away any stray blobs of wax with a lint-free cloth. And that's it – job done.

APPLYING DARK WAX FOR A VINTAGE PATINA

If you want a little more patina, there's a fabulous range of tinted waxes that can be rubbed into corners and carved details and then rubbed off, leaving just enough shading to add some faux vintage patina. There's only one caveat: *never* apply dark wax directly onto unwaxed chalk-painted furniture. The porous paint surface will soak up the dark pigments, leaving a horrible stain that you can't remove. Instead, apply a coat of clear wax first and then, while the clear wax is still moist and freshly applied to the surface, apply your dark wax (I always use dark brown) with a brush or a soft lint-free cloth, making sure you get it into all the cracks and crevices you want to highlight. Once this is done, quickly wipe off all the excess wax using a soft cloth, or brush the surface with some clear wax. The clear wax acts almost like a cleaning agent, stripping back as much or as little of the dark wax as you desire. I tend to opt for a more subtle patina, so one technique I've developed is to mix 1–2 teaspoons of dark brown wax with 1–2 tablespoons of clear wax (using an old spoon and a little jam jar). If you apply this slightly diluted dark brown wax it will give you a much more subtle effect, which you can build on if necessary.

LIME WASH MASONRY PAINT

I first discovered lime wash paint when I visited Bauwerk Colour in Fremantle, Western Australia, more than ten years ago, and I've been using their paint ever since. It's not only their range of alluring colours that I find so beguiling. Their paints are made from 100 per cent natural ingredients and pigments, which produce the most beautiful, nuanced patina and luminosity on masonry walls, with the paint being absorbed by, and becoming part of, the wall itself.

One thing that we as paint consumers need to understand is that even if we buy low or zero VOC (volatile organic compound), 'eco-friendly', conventional paint, it's still made from plastics and chemicals – which wash away into our water supply. Although I can't imagine I'd ever stop using conventional paints for woodwork and for plasterboard walls, I love the fact that when I use Bauwerk paints I know that everything that goes down the drain once came from the earth. The paints are literally made using earthen pigments, clay, minerals and water, in a 100 per cent green-powered production process. For this reason, they're safe and non-polluting. Because Bauwerk paints have no plastic content, they allow walls to breathe, thereby increasing air transfer, reducing humidity and adding to a more stable ambient temperature within buildings. The natural antifungal properties of the lime in the paint keep mould at bay, which is a great bonus for allergy sufferers and asthmatics.

I used Bauwerk in colour Bone on the island bench in the barn; it's almost an exact match with the grey-beige render and the joins in the stone walls. What's lovely about this paint is that it will always dry with a soft, nuanced finish. You won't be able to exactly match a Bauwerk paint to another colour in the room – but it will stand together as one with the comparable colour while succeeding alone on its own merits. I could have left the grey-beige render on the island bench, but it marks easily; matched in Bauwerk, the surface retains its ability to breathe and remains as close as possible to the natural texture of the render. And I can apply a fresh coat of paint at any time in the future in less than thirty minutes, making it a very serviceable masonry treatment for high-traffic kitchen areas prone to scuffs and splatters.

For the barn fireplace, I used the Bauwerk colour Catkin. The fireplace surround was built half out of masonry and stone and half out of fire-rated plasterboard. Although Bauwerk is ideally suited to masonry, you can also paint it onto plasterboard; because our plasterboard was new, I painted the Bauwerk straight on, without an undercoat. If there are different substrates in your wall, you may see a subtle variation in the colour or even a slight 'ghosting' (white patches on the surface) if you apply the lime wash paint without first sealing the wall (I use Bauwerk's undercoat). Gloss or semi-gloss painted walls should always be sandpapered before applying Bauwerk paint.

Bauwerk sell two types of brushes for lime wash: one with a red plastic handle and natural bristles, and another with a wooden handle and slightly softer natural bristles. The red-handled brush is ideal for masonry, but if you're painting onto plasterboard I'd recommend the wooden-handled brush, which will give you a much softer, less textured result.

THERE IS ALWAYS A SEASONING TRAY NEXT TO THE STOVE IN MY KITCHEN, COMPLETE WITH: TWO
TYPES OF SALT, THE COARSE GREY *GROS SEL DE GUÉRANDE* AND A LOCAL *FLEUR DE SEL* FROM
SALLIES-DE-BÉARN; A VASE OF FRESH HERBS, PICKED DAILY; COOKING AND DRESSING OILS; AND
AN EVER-CHANGING ASSORTMENT OF FRESHLY ROASTED AND GROUND SPICE MIXES. HAVING
THESE AT YOUR FINGERTIPS ALLOWS YOU TO BE MORE SPONTANEOUS AND INTUITIVE WITH
SEASONAL PRODUCE, PARTICULARLY WHEN YOU HAVE A GLUT OF ONE PARTICULAR VEGETABLE
THAT DEMANDS A VARIETY OF COOKING METHODS AND FLAVOUR TREATMENTS.

119

Bauwerk lime wash paints

1. LAKE 2. BONE 3. CATKIN 4. TWEED 5. TURNIP 6. HAZELNUT

7. WOLF 8. ARTEMISIA 9. CARDAMOM 10. NETTLE 11. HEAVY FROST 12. KELP

How to apply Bauwerk Colour lime wash paint

1. Lime wash paint is surprisingly watery compared with normal paint – so when you are ready to use your paint, give it a good shake and stir, ensuring that all the pigments and solid bits at the bottom are well blended. Once the paint is mixed, I like to pour half the quantity into another bucket and paint directly from that. One other thing I'd add is that, because it's a natural product with natural pigments, it can have a slightly 'natural', almost algae-like smell when you open the tin; this is not at all unpleasant – it just doesn't smell like regular paint. Any aroma will disappear completely once the lime wash is dry.

2. I always apply lime wash paint with my special wooden-handled paintbrush – I bought mine from Bauwerk many years ago and it's still going strong. The beauty of these brushes is their natural bristles. To ensure you get the best from your brush, dip it into the lime wash and then give it a good flick into the bucket to remove any excess paint. If you do this, the bristles will retain just the right amount of paint, which they will release in an even coat as you brush across the wall or other surface.

3. Apply the paint in crisscross brushstrokes from one corner of the wall, working outwards from the wet edge, avoiding creating any drips. The objective is *not* to be tempted to apply the paint too thickly; if you do, it will result in poor bonding and powdering when dry.

4. It is best to apply lime-based paints in thin layers, gradually building opacity as you go. Two to three coats are recommended to achieve the true depth of colour.

Note: If you've ordered a selection of Bauwerk samples and don't want to waste them, paint them directly onto a collection of terracotta pots – this paint is perfect for plant pots. The colours add a beautiful pop to garden terraces and kitchen benchtops, too.

POTS PAINTED WITH BAUWERK LIME WASH.
FROM LEFT TO RIGHT: CARDAMOM, KELP, ARTEMISIA, NETTLE, LAKE.

FRENCH COUNTRY PATTERN

WITHIN SECONDS OF WALKING IN my front door it will be pretty clear to visitors that I'm a lover of surface design: fabrics, wallpapers, rugs … I adore them all. What I love most is their ability to inject character and add a sense of rhythm to a room through pattern. French country is all about creating a layered aesthetic that's elegant but understated, and the curation of patterns is a great tool for introducing that extra layer of interest. They keep the eye engaged while at the same time leading it to other contrasting features in the room, like a plain linen sofa or sisal rug.

Pattern can also take you on the most wonderful adventures. There's no doubt where you'll land surrounded by toile designs, but a little bit of chinoiserie, like the design used in the tall tower bedroom, might just take you to a 19th-century bohemian boudoir in a chic Bordelaise town-house – or even the Orient, if you choose a design with the odd monkey or exotic bird.

I see pattern as the illustration in a story of your telling. The plain colours in the room act as the text, but your story can be as colourful and complexly layered as you choose to make it. It's the little touches of the unexpected that will bring that certain *je ne sais quoi* to your interior. Don't forget that the interplay of a stripe or check can sometimes be pattern's very best friend.

Pattern can be striking, subtle and everything in between, so there's something for everyone in this category. But if it suits you, be bold, be playful!

WALLPAPER

Wallpaper has a wonderful way of wrapping you in colour and pattern. To my mind, it produces the same effect as musical notes on a page of sheet music. While you can't hear a tune simply by looking at the printed quavers and crotchets, you can feel the rhythm of the notes carrying you away to imaginary places full of whimsy and wonder. The colour and pattern of wallpaper have this same ability to transport you – it's simply up to you to choose where.

Have a look at the lists you made for your feel board and think about how they might influence your choice of pattern. There will be wonderful clues guiding you towards the designs that resonate with you most strongly. Think about the colours you've listed and the way they make you feel. Wallpaper can be a wonderful medium to unite playful design with multiple colours, but if bold pattern is a bit overwhelming, why not consider a smaller, more discreet design or a plain embossed paper that can be painted in a colour from the commercial or NCS colour palettes in the previous chapter. Embossed papers allow you to have the pattern that comes with wallpaper, just very quietly, with a lovely subtle texture to add interest to your selected colour.

The general rule for wallpaper patterns is fairly straightforward: the bigger the design, the more dominating it becomes, making larger rooms feel smaller. This can be a great thing for overwhelmingly large spaces with high ceilings (our ceilings are just over 3 metres high) or for bedrooms that would otherwise feel too cold and uninviting. But, by the same token, a large, bold print can make smaller rooms with low ceilings look positively squat. One thing I like to do in some of our smaller rooms (bear in mind, though, that the ceilings are still high) is combine slightly larger designs with painted timber panelling, to reduce the risk of the design dominating the space and acting like a rather bossy, headstrong prima donna.

If you're a little apprehensive about using wallpaper and it's your first time, the more subtle patterns might suit you best. Wallpaper choices are literally endless – but to show you how I selected my papers, I've included some of the designs I considered for a few of the rooms in my house. I recommend ordering a few sample colourways of the same design; if a design speaks to you, it can be fun to play with it in a few of your favourite colours. You can see this in my collage of French toile (p. 139), where I experimented with three colours of the same Little Greene Revolution Stag Toile (and eventually settled on the blue).

Another thing I highly recommend is to take a *really* good look at the wallpaper colours you've selected by arranging them all together on a surface. Notice how certain colours sit next to one another. There will be some lovely clues here that could guide you from a wallpaper to the choice of a colour for an adjoining room. For example, I love red and blue, so when I chose Little Greene High Street Rouge wallpaper for the stairwell, I juxtaposed it with a blue-coloured paint in the bedroom (Little Greene Juniper Ash) – giving depth and cosy intimacy to what is rather a small bedroom while at the same time showing off the fabulous red Les Indiennes design of the wallpaper in all its glory. Likewise, it contrasts with the inky blue of Farrow & Ball Hague Blue in my husband's study on the ground floor. The bedroom on the other side at the top of the stairwell is painted in Ressource Grey, and at the base of the stairwell the wallpaper contrasts with a lower section of plain wall in Farrow & Ball Mole's Breath. I chose to put a wooden moulding on the wall so that the wallpaper didn't continue all the way to the ground. The stairwell is very tall and the Les Indiennes tree of life design is a very upward-leading vertical pattern, so this gave the lower level a feeling of being grounded and slightly cosier. Always consider the colour and pattern of an adjoining room, particularly if you're using two different wallpapers that can be seen from the same viewpoint (this was the case in the barn, where the hallway wallpaper can be seen with the green bedroom wallpaper). As long as the colours don't compete and the size of the designs is harmonious, your choices will generally be fine, but it's often helpful to tape samples to the walls and live with them for a week or so, just to be sure.

LEFT: THERE IS SOMETHING SIMPLE YET ACHINGLY ELEGANT ABOUT A DEDICATED DRINKS TABLE. OURS ALWAYS CARRIES A BASKET OF NUTS COMPLETE WITH MY GRANDFATHER'S OLD BRASS NUT CRACKERS; A SIMPLE COCKTAIL NIBBLE THAT'S ALWAYS ON HAND, BUT ONE YOU HAVE TO WORK FOR – MY TAKE ON SLOW SNACKING!

CENTRE: A PILE OF OLD BOOKS MAKES A PERFECT PLINTH FOR MY OLD BROWNIE BOX CAMERA,
A STRING OF ANTIQUE ROSARY BEADS (FOUND IN A DRAWER) AND A PORCELAIN OWL FROM AUSTRALIA.

RIGHT: THE BLUE BEDROOM IN THE BARN. I DISGUISED THE UGLY ALUMINIUM SLIDING
MECHANISM OF THE DOOR WITH A CARVED WOODEN PELMET.

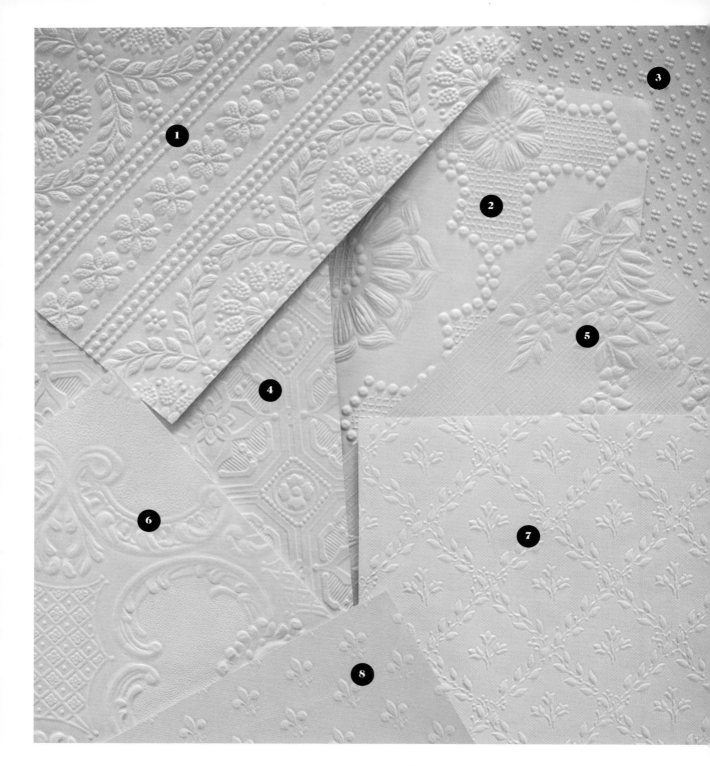

Embossed

NOTE: ALL WALLPAPERS FROM ANAGLYPTA WALLPAPERS.

1. TOWNSEND/STRIPE RD340   2. ALEXANDER RD0647   3. CHURCHILL/FLORAL RD385   4. DERBY/CLASSICAL RD124
5. PORTLAND/FLORAL RD341   6. ALFRED RD0137   7. HAMNETT/FLORAL RD393   8. TUDOR/CLASSICAL RD392

Embossed wallpapers

I love embossed papers, the way they add subtle texture and pattern. Embossed wallpapers look wonderful above or below a chair rail (also known as a dado rail) detail; they bring a gentle visual difference that 'breaks up' a wall, with or without introducing a change in colour.

The designs shown opposite (which all date from the late 19th century) can be painted with regular wall paint to suit the function of the room and can be embossed by the manufacturers onto a variety of papers, to fulfil a range of uses: from traditional crisp, pure paper for living rooms, ceilings and bedrooms, to modern vinyls and super-tough reinforced textile papers for bathrooms and high-traffic areas such as stairwells. Any colour from the commercial palettes or my NCS palettes would look beautiful painted over one of these embossed papers – which are also particularly handsome with white or darker, moodier shades in a flat paint finish.

WALLPAPERING TIPS

Wallpapering is not my favourite task. The wallpapers I tend to choose are a sizeable chunk of my decorating budget, so mistakes can be rather costly, particularly if I'm the one holding the scissors! For this reason, I prefer to use a professional. These days you can find reliable wallpaper calculators online, and if you're wanting to get a feel for the cost of the paper itself you can easily measure walls and enter the dimensions into the calculator for a rough guide to how many rolls you will need; however, it's always best to consult a professional in order to sure up the price (including the cost of glue and labour).

Depending on the length of the pattern repeat, the height of your walls and how the pattern is matched (straight matched or drop matched), your requirements could alter quite a bit. There can be a lot of waste with patterns as opposed to simpler designs such as stripes.

It would take a whole other book to explain pattern matching, the techniques for paste-to-the-wall vs traditional paste-to-paper methods and general how-to-wallpaper instructions. Fortunately, there are excellent tutorials available online, so I suggest that budding DIY wallpaper fans watch a few videos.

Botanical and animal prints

If you love nature, bring it inside. I'm an obsessive gardener, and I'm also a bird lover. At the ripe old age of nine, I cut out the stork logo from a Japan Airlines ad, glued it onto a piece of paper as a letterhead and wrote to Sydney's Taronga Zoo as the self-appointed president (and only member) of the Junior Bird League of Australia, offering my expert services to the head bird keeper. Miraculously, he wrote back and let me volunteer on weekends, feeding beautiful baby macaws and rhea chicks, and checking eggs in the incubators; he even gave me an aviary for my backyard to raise orphaned magpies and currawongs. From that moment on, there have always been birds in my home – as well as collections of feathers, mantelpieces scattered with abandoned bird's nests and, of course, bird-inspired wallpaper.

The botanical design that I chose for the dining room (Zoffany Eleonora Ref GUV08003) starts from the timber panelling at thigh height. I painted the panelling in a colour I mixed myself to match the branches in the wallpaper, using Autentico Dark Pepper with a little tint of a brown that I found in the hardware store – not recommended by the manufacturer, but I'm a bit of a rebel; it's still holding strong after four years, so I have to assume it's okay. This darker colour at the base gives a feeling of depth, grounding the botanical design and making the room feel more naturally like a forest, with solid trunks below, and foliage and branches above. The vertical, serpentine design of the branches on a paler background evokes a lovely feeling of life, light and movement, leading the eye towards the beams (painted in Farrow & Ball Cornforth White, with Strong White in between). Although the overall result creates a tangible sense of spaciousness and height, the dining room still feels cosy, anchored by the painted panels. The room is a space we use for informal family meals by the fire as well as for elegant formal dinner parties; it feels neither too casual nor too precious. If your ceiling is of standard height (2.43 to 2.74 metres), this can be a good way to create the illusion that the walls are taller than they actually are.

I've kept my use of botanical prints in the house primarily within a group of patterns known as Les Indiennes, which have a long history in France. I've also used Swedish patterns – which sit beautifully within my colour palette because of the design history linking France and Sweden – as well as toile wallpaper, which generally depicts a landscape scene with people or animals.

Botanical and animal prints

1. LITTLE GREENE, BRODSWORTH, CONSORT **2.** MORRIS & CO., MARY ISOBEL 214730
3. PIERRE FREY, BRAQUENIÉ ANN-MARIE ORIGINAL BP317001 **4.** SANDBERG, EUGEN 413-21
5. LITTLE GREENE, WHITEHALL, PRUSSIAN **6.** PIERRE FREY, SANS PAPILLONS, BEIGE
7. LITTLE GREENE, DARWIN, AZURE **8.** PIERRE FREY, BRAQUENIÉ LA FONTAINE, CHARCOAL/TAUPE
9. SANDBERG, ROSENHOLM 407-62 **10.** PIERRE FREY, BRAQUENIÉ BENGALI, OCHRE BP203005

Dominos

NOTE: ALL WALLPAPERS FROM ANTOINETTE POISSON.
1. JAÏPUR, BLEU ET VERT 57B **2.** BAIES, BLEU ET VERT 56B **3.** OLIVES, VERT 55A **4.** JARDIN, VERT 39A
5. GRENADES, N&B 2B **6.** OISEAUX & FEUILLAGE, 24A **7.** RUBANS & OISEAUX, BLEU 54B
8. JAÏPUR, MULTICOLOR 57A

Domino papers

Domino papers were the precursors of wallpaper as we know it today. They were originally printed using handcarved wooden blocks on single sheets of paper (usually 32 x 42 centimetres), then handpainted or stencilled using natural pigments and gum arabic. Reaching the height of their popularity in the 18th century, they were produced in vast quantities and sold at an affordable price, which made them popular adornments for furniture and small rooms that otherwise would have been too costly to decorate. Placed side by side, domino papers created a continuous, repetitive pattern perfect for dressing the walls of small corridors or servants' quarters, as well as the insides of hat boxes, travelling chests, wardrobes and cabinets. They were even used in the binding of books and brochures.

Traditionally overseen by artisan 'dominotiers' – expert printers who sometimes also made playing cards – the craft of domino paper production has recently been revived by Vincent Farelly and Jean-Baptiste Martin, both heritage restorers specialising in wallpaper. They are the co-founders and artistic directors of A Paris chez Antoinette Poisson, a domino paper production and retail house named in homage to the Marquise de Pompadour – born Jeanne-Antoinette Poisson – a renowned devotee of the decorative arts. Their range of individual domino papers are faithfully produced by hand using traditional techniques and make beautiful wall art, simply framed and hung in a collection as a gallery of exquisite designs. Antoinette Poisson also produce a select range of domino designs as wallpaper by the roll.

Gustavian / Swedish

NOTE: ALL WALLPAPERS FROM SANDBERG WALLPAPER.
1. AXEL GREEN **2.** KAROLINA BLUE **3.** KARL BLUE **4.** SIGFRID BLUE
5. EDVIN MISTY BLUE **6.** EWA GREY **7.** VIOLA BLUE
8. GUSTAV LIGHT BLUE **9.** EDVIN WILLOW GREEN

A QUICK HISTORY OF GUSTAVIAN COLOUR

Like a great many visitors to the palace of Versailles, King Gustav III of Sweden (who lived from 1746 to 1792) was rather starstruck and took home a number of ideas; one of which led to a colour palette known today as 'Gustavian'. It's essentially the same as the soft, slightly muted palette you see here in the landscape of the Béarn and on the shutters and doors of local villages: pale greens, blues, soft pinks, greys and slightly dirty whites. Rather than the showy extravagance of Versailles, Gustav III opted for an elegant, restrained palette, with chroma-reduced colours, muted and slightly washed out with grey.

There's also a rather interesting coincidence that forms a further bond between Sweden and the Béarn. Just twenty-six years after Gustav III's death, a Frenchman from the Béarn, Jean Baptiste Bernadotte, became king of Sweden. Bernadotte, who was born in Pau, had been a general in the French imperial army. At Emperor Napoleon's rather insistent behest, Bernadotte was adopted by the dying King Charles XIII of Sweden, and he acceded to the throne in 1818, ruling as Charles XIV John, king of Sweden and Norway. It's through him that the current Swedish royal family are descended, so by virtue of this local connection, I think it's only fitting that I have a few Swedish wallpapers in the house too.

THE TOILE BATHROOM. THE WINDOWSILL WAS INSTALLED BY OUR LOCAL STONEMASON AND MAKES USE OF A PIECE OF SALVAGED MARBLE I FOUND AT A RECLAMATION YARD. THE REMAINDER OF THE FIXTURES ARE ALL ORIGINAL, WITH THE EXCEPTION OF THE VANITY LIGHT AND THE WALLPAPER.

Toile de Jouy

1. PIERRE FREY, PP SEPTEUIL, PINK-RED B02 **2.** LITTLE GREENE, STAG TOUILE, JUNIPER
3. COLE & SON, VILLANDRY 99/1003 **4.** LITTLE GREENE, STAG TOUILE, CHOCOLATE
5. LITTLE GREENE, STAG TOUILE, BURGUNDY **6.** PIERRE FREY, COUTANCES, NATURAL FP195001
7. PIERRE FREY, CRESPIERE, ROSE ANCIEN FP170002 **8.** PIERRE FREY, COUTANCES, WHEAT FP195003
9. COLE & SON, VERSAILLES 99/15061 **10.** HARLEQUIN, ETIENNE 60104

FABRIC

I tend to put my pattern on the walls; so, for this reason, the fabrics I choose are often rustic linens and hemp in plain colours. But if there is no wallpaper, or if the wallpaper design is subtle, I will use casual florals and stripes that don't compete for too much attention and that blend well with the colours of adjoining rooms.

The general rule of thumb for choosing a fabric pattern is to start by deciding what your pattern hero will be. If, for example, the 'hero' is a boldly patterned rug, like a kilim, then complement it with plain fabrics and furnishings that allow it to be the star. If you want a more dramatic, eclectic, eccentric or bohemian feel, then you can layer more pattern, adding interest to plain surfaces with textural effects such as fringing, velvets or deep-pile rugs. Pattern on pattern can certainly work – in fact, it's fabulous if you're a big personality and want to express various elements from your feel board in the same room. Use what resonates with you most strongly, and imagine the way you'd feel if you were wearing all the patterns at once in an ensemble. If you'd walk out the door wearing them, feeling like they were *you*, then go for it!

For the confident use of patterned fabric, you only have to look at a classic style often seen in French boudoirs (typically women's private bedrooms), where one fabric, usually a toile de Jouy, is applied to upholstered walls, bedhead, bed linen, armchairs, curtains and cushions, resulting in a very intentional repetition of the pattern on almost every surface. The result is unquestionably extravagant, opulent and fabulously old-French.

Toile de Jouy

'Toile' is the French word for canvas or linen cloth, but it is more commonly used to refer specifically to toile de Jouy. This is a patterned fabric, usually with an off-white background, depicting scenes of rural life in a single colour – traditionally red, blue or black (although the colour range expanded as the style became more popular from the early 1800s onwards). Toile de Jouy was first made in the late 18th century in Jouy-en-Josas, a commune in the south-western suburbs of Paris. Although Toile de Jouy is specifically a fabric, 'toile' is now often used to refer generally to the pattern type.

I've used toile in one of the bathrooms as well as a bedroom, both as wallpaper and as fabric. (Having said that … for me, a little bit of toile goes a long way. I'm not a fan of toile on every surface, I find it just a bit too much.) Toile also makes a lovely traditional French-style bedhead canopy, which can be hung from an antique wooden *ciel de lit*. Literally meaning 'sky of the bed', this is a carved canopy frame (similar to a small drapery or upholstered curtain sconce) that conceals the curtain hooks and rail and forms a little crown above the bed, from which the curtains hang on either side of the mattress. You

THE TOILE ROOM.

can find these frames via antique sites online or at French *brocantes* and antique shops. I love the carved wooden ones, painted in chalk-based paint.

The antique toile fabric used in my daughter's room was found in an old armoire on the first floor. It was originally four short curtains, but on a visit from Australia my dear mother – a master seamstress – managed to piece them into two curtains with a little left over for a cushion and silk-fringed tie-backs (found in an old box in the attic). Fascinated to find out more about the toile's origins, I sent my French antique fabric guru Nicole Fabre some photos, which she promptly identified as 'Les Fables de la Fontaine', printed circa 1805 by Oberkampf Manufacture Royale at Jouy-en-Josas. As with every real-life renovation – and by that I mean the ones that happen over time as funds become available – these curtains will eventually be lined and made a little fuller with a solid linen panel on each side of the toile. For now, they stand tall and live another day as simple curtains, a mere 215 years after the day they rolled off the printing table.

Les Indiennes

As the name suggests, these fabrics were inspired by Indian textiles, which became extremely popular in France during the 17th, 18th and 19th centuries – so much so that their manufacture and importation were prohibited by royal decree in 1686, in order to protect the hard-hit local French silk and wool industries. Despite this prohibition, Les Indiennes fabrics continued to be produced illicitly, particularly in Marseille, until they were legalised in 1759.

Les Indiennes were traditionally made using natural vegetable dyes that produced beautiful reds, pinks, yellows and blues. Reds and pinks came from the madder plant, *Rubia tinctorum* (*garance* in French); yellows from weld or dyer's mignonette, *Reseda luteola* (*gaude*) and blues from woad, *Isatis tinctoria* (*pastel des teinturiers*). The Béarn was once part of the *trail du pastel des teinturiers*, a trading route along the Pyrénées that ran from the wealthy woad merchant cites of Albi, Carcassonne and Toulouse to Bordeaux and Bayonne – where the woad was exported to Spain, England and elsewhere in Europe.

I've included here a beautiful selection of contemporary Les Indiennes designs that I collected when sourcing fabrics for the house, but you can find many more via fabric houses listed in the sourcing guide. Some of the patterns can be quite large, which is great if you have high ceilings for long curtain drops that will show off a bold fabric design to its best advantage; but if your ceiling height is standard or low, it's best to opt for smaller designs that are less prone to overwhelming the room. One of the recurring motifs you'll see in Les Indiennes designs is the tree of life, which features in the Little Greene wallpaper I used in the stairwell. Not only is it a beautiful design, but its fruits and bare branches also represent the cycle of life and rebirth, a lovely thing to be reminded of each time you climb the stairs, particularly after a trying day!

I also adore Indian woodblock fabrics. They give a respectful nod to the history of French 'Indiennes', but they also bring a bit a wanderlust to my interiors and remind me of my travels in Nepal and India.

ORGANIC HEMP TRAY NAPKIN, BY COULEUR CHANVRE, SAINT-JEAN-DE-LUZ, AND BED LINEN, WITH CAÏ FAHREL WOODBLOCK PRINT.

Les Indiennes

1. PUKKA PRINT, SPRIG, CLAY & FLINT **2.** PUKKA PRINT, POM, CLAY & FLINT **3.** CAÏ FAHREL, DAHLIA, INDIGO
4. PUKKA PRINT, MARI, RED & ROSE **5.** PUKKA PRINT, FLORAL JAAL, BLUSH & BLOSSOM
6. CAÏ FAHREL, SNAIL, CHARCOAL **7.** PUKKA PRINT, POSY, CRIMSON & DOVE BLUE **8.** PUKKA PRINT, SCALLOP, RED & ROSE
9. PUKKA PRINT, ALL OVER, BLUE & RED **10.** PUKKA PRINT, TENDRIL, BLUSH & AQUA
11. PUKKA FABRE, PETITE FLEUR, INDIGO **12.** PUKKA FABRE, PETITE FLEUR, ROSE

Traditional Indian woodblock fabrics are still being produced by the Khatri and Chippa communities in Gujarat and Rajasthan. The artisanal process of carving the designs onto seasoned sheesham timber blocks called *bunta* gives them a beautiful, raw connection with both the earth and also the human hands that are part of the process at every stage of their production. Each colour in the design has its own block. The *rekh* is the outline block. The next block to be applied is the *gudh*, which forms the background. *Datta* blocks are used to infill the design.

I particularly love the fabrics produced by Juliet Cornell's Indian-based block-printing company Pukka Print (as well as Pukka Print's collection with Nicole Fabre and John Laflin, called Pukka Fabre).

The designs hark back to many of the original Les Indiennes fabrics from the 1700s, but are beautifully reinterpreted in scale, pattern and colour to produce Anglo/French/Indian designs that fit perfectly within my interiors.

Caï Fahrel, headed by the talented Sacha Leppard, produces another woodblock range from Rajasthan; a collection I adore for its whimsical botanical designs and muted colour palette printed on beautiful hand-loomed linen. Their block-printed, hand-stitched quilts, made with pure cotton wadding, are on almost every bed in my house. Sacha's latest collection experiments with the traditional Indian 'Ajrakh' resist print method that uses clay and natural vegetable dyes made from pomegranate, turmeric and indigo.

Plains

Every pattern needs a place to rest. Consider plains the canvas for your choice of fabric 'illustration'; for example, a plain-coloured sofa with patterned scatter cushions or a plain-coloured wall for a patterned curtain. My staple palette of plain fabrics is all French, all of them made with totally natural materials: cotton, linen, hemp … the more raw the better. I use these fabrics for chair and sofa slipcovers (fabulously practical with children and dogs), cushions, fixed upholstery, curtains and bed linen.

When it comes to linen and hemp, the price point can vary enormously, starting with cheap yet serviceable plains (IKEA do a great natural linen, as does Bouchara, a French homewares store) and going on to become eye-wateringly expensive when you buy a quality hand-loomed product that is organically grown and dyed. My advice is to buy what you can afford; but if you only want to buy bed linen once, invest in quality – it will literally last a lifetime and becomes better with age. I use Couleur Chanvre, a local company from Saint-Jean-de-Luz that has developed a unique dye process for their 100 per cent organic, 100 per cent French-grown and manufactured textiles, which are made from hemp, cotton and flax fibre. Their dyeing process excludes the traditional toxic dye primers and chemical products (endocrine disruptors, allergens and irritants) that are used in almost all textile industries. When you buy organic linen or cotton, it's important to understand that it may indeed have been *grown* organically – which is great for the planet – but the dyeing process can completely negate the benefits to your health and the environment. It's like buying organic tomatoes and making a dressing with toxic chemicals.

145

Bio Denim Nizza - 15.9 OZ -
145 cm - GOTS zertifiziert
durch CERES-076 Blau
Art.Nr.: E-D-191

Denim and chambray

NOTE: ALL FABRICS BY LEBENSKLEIDUNG.
1. BIO CHAMBRAY 120 G/M2 NATUR BLAU **2.** BIO CANVAS 290 G/M2 NATURAL
3. BIO CANVAS 280 G/M2 WHITE **4.** BIO DENIM NIZZA 15.9 OZ BLAU

Couleur Chanvre's organic linen is grown by the Terre de Lin cooperative in Normandy. It's the linen I use for plain cushions, napkins and table runners. When it comes to bed linen, I prefer their pure hemp. It's beautifully comfortable and soft, but also naturally antibacterial, hypo-allergenic and antifungal. The hollow fibres of hemp act like a natural thermostat, and it wasn't until I started sleeping between these sheets that I realised quite how effective they were. Hemp is never cold in winter or hot in summer and, contrary to what you might expect, it's not scratchy and raw – it's luxuriously soft and gets softer with lifelong use. The heavier style of hemp is wonderful for upholstery. I've used it on the bed in the tall tower bedroom, trimmed with rustic bronze studs. Teamed with hemp sheets (all the colours in the Couleur Chanvre range go beautifully together), it adds a touch of raw 'rural' texture to what is a rather pretty French boudoir featuring Little Greene Darwin Azure wallpaper.

Denim and chambray

Denim, that hard-wearing French cotton fabric originally made for use in work clothes, also has a tie with India; its predecessor, dungaree, has been produced there for hundreds of years. However, the product we know today as denim was first made in the French city of Nîmes under the name *serge de Nîmes*.

I love using denim for slipcovers – white denim is perfect for this. It's also great for chair upholstery if you want to inject a little bit of indigo into your colour palette. If you're handy with a sewing machine, you can make cushion covers using salvaged fabric from unwanted jeans and denim shirts. It's a nice reference in a French country interior; both because it's the perfect shade of indigo and because it's a fabric of French origin that was invented primarily to clothe manual labourers.

Like denim, chambray is made with a blue and white warp/weft weave; but chambray is a plain weave, whereas denim is a twill. Chambray is generally a lighter weight fabric (although you can find thicker versions), and is the same colour on both sides. This makes chambray better suited for curtains, cushions and general soft furnishings. Chambray dates back as far as the 16th century, originating from Cambrai in northern France, where it was used to make high-quality linen cloth, shirting, handkerchiefs and even intricate lacework. I love the soft duck-egg hue of natural blue chambray; it's the perfect French blue in my opinion. I buy mine from German producer Lebenskleidung – admittedly not French, but a sustainable, planet-focused company that also makes a range of organically grown denim, twill and canvas suitable for slipcovers and soft furnishings.

Basque fabric

The term 'Basque fabric' is a little bit contentious today – and a little dangerous, because the border between the Béarn and the Pays Basque is just a few kilometres from our house; something that's certainly never in doubt when it comes to the fierce loyalty these two regions each have for their unique patrimony. Today only two of the original manufacturers of Basque fabric remain. Both are located in the Béarn, and have been from their inception: Lartigue, which was founded in 1910 in Oloron-Sainte-Marie; and Tissage Moutet, founded in 1919 in Orthez. Both continue the tradition of making beautiful striped Basque fabrics as well as jacquard cotton, espadrille fabric and fabric sold by the metre for napery, deckchairs, upholstery, curtains, cushions and a whole range of homewares and accessories.

These fabrics are known as 'Basque' for the pattern that was originally woven into the heavy white flax linen, in the form of seven red and green stripes. These stripes denoted the seven provinces that still make up the Pays Basque: three in France and four in Spain. Red, green and white proudly remain the colours of the Basque region.

Traditionally, the striped heavy-weave cloth was made into blankets for the oxen that ploughed the fields. As an Australian, I initially found this idea utterly perplexing. When I politely asked why cows would need to wear little coats to work, I was told in a very matter-of-fact way by a Basque farmer that it was 'obviously' to protect them from heatstroke and flies. I can't imagine why this never caught on in Australia!

It wasn't long before the famous Basque stripe found its way from the domain of animal husbandry to homewares and began to be used by Basque farmers' wives for tablecloths and a range of other textile accessories. As time progressed, the traditional red, white and green stripe was replaced by brightly coloured designs that now define the beach tents, deckchairs, tables, espadrilles and homewares of the Côte Basques.

There are now numerous manufacturers selling both the traditional stripe and their own versions of the fabric in the busy streets of Basque towns like Saint-Jean-de-Luz, Bayonne and Biarritz. You can also strike a great bargain at the factory shops of Lartigue (who after recent restructuring are now calling themselves Lartigue 1910), in Ascain, and Tissage Moutet, still based in Orthez. Both make a coated version – a bit like oilcloth – of their canvas fabrics, which is great for outdoor furniture, or for tablecloths that can be wiped down after meals with a soapy cloth (if you're like me and have young, messy eaters).

AN ARRAY OF STRIPED BASQUE COTTON, CANVAS AND ESPADRILLE FABRICS FROM LARTIGUE 1910 AND TISSAGE MOUTET, WHICH CAN BE PURCHASED BY THE METRE. BOTH COMPANIES MAKE A COATED VERSION THAT IS VERY SERVICEABLE FOR TABLECLOTHS AND APRONS.

Trims and fringes

1. FRINGE MARKET, CHAINETTE SKIRT FRINGE, SPA 2. FRINGE MARKET, FRILLS TASSEL FRINGE, ICE
3. HOULÈS, FLEURS DE LIN, COL. 9000 4. FRINGE MARKET, BOHEMIAN FRINGE, OUTDOOR SKYE 5. FRINGE MARKET, BIJOUX 4 IN
WIDE GIMP, FRENCHIE 6. FRINGE MARKET, CHEVRON WOOL, ICE 7. FRINGE MARKET, BATTENBERG LACE, ROSE
8. FRINGE MARKET, CHEVRON WOOL, FOG 9. FRINGE MARKET, 3 BELL TASSEL FRINGE, SONOMA
10. FRINGE MARKET, CIRCUS FRINGE, NAVY 11. FRINGE MARKET, 3 BELL TASSEL FRINGE, FRENCH FARMHOUSE
12. FRINGE MARKET, BATTENBERG LACE, BURGUNDY 13. HOULÈS, FLEURS DE LIN, COL. 9825
14. FRINGE MARKET, CHEVRON WOOL, OCEAN 15. FRINGE MARKET, FRILLS TASSEL FRINGE, PEACOCK
16. FRINGE MARKET, FRILLS TASSEL FRINGE, COASTAL LIVING 17. FRINGE MARKET, VINTAGE WEBBING, AMERICANA 1
18. FRINGE MARKET, VINTAGE WEBBING, AMERICANA 5 19. FRINGE MARKET, VINTAGE WEBBING, WINTER 1

La passementerie

Who doesn't love a fringe, pom-pom or a bit of braid to finish upholstery and curtains? Nobody does it as well as the French – take Houlès, for example, who have been making exquisite trimmings since 1928 (several other manufacturers are listed in the sourcing guide).

A word of warning about tassels and other trimmings: like any pretty bauble, they sometimes come with a considerable price tag, particularly if you require large quantities. For this reason I tend to use them on smaller items, like lampshades and cushions.

Vintage fabrics and linen are a great way to add texture. I love old French curtains; some of the originals from the house still hang in the bedrooms. Grain sacks have sadly become a bit expensive and clichéd in my opinion (if things become a trend, I tend to fall out of love with them, quickly) – though they truly are beautiful. I have a number of them that I use as table runners.

One thing that I do collect with a passion is antique French linen. Beautiful old linen and hemp sheets, tea towels, bedspreads, napkins, handtowels and aprons. Perhaps my most prized find was a stack of linen aprons – long ones that tie around the waist – which I discovered at the back of an old armoire on the first floor. They once belonged to the long-gone maid who lived at the top of the tower in the attic; it's fascinating to imagine what life must have been like back then. These old linens are often monogrammed, adding a historical detail that gives French country interiors another layer of provenance.

TEXTURAL ELEMENTS

Texture is key when it comes to determining the amount of 'country' you include in your version of French country. Bringing in raw, textured and rustic elements can help to dial down the chintz of *passementerie* and other 'prettier' elements – which in the presence of sleek, tailored materials can feel formal and a bit more 'château' than 'country cottage'.

Setting 'pretty' features against unpainted wooden furniture and architectural details, such as old, matt-finished oak floorboards, wooden shelving and salvaged oak doors, or rustic stone finishes, like tumbled travertine marble tiles, old *tomettes* (terracotta tiles) and stone walls and window/door surrounds, really accentuates each element's virtues. Woven natural fibres also offer a rustic counterpart to fine woven trims – wicker baskets, Thonet bentwood chairs with woven cane seats, basket-style pendant lighting, hessian fabric and seagrass matting all work beautifully. Essentially, the further from synthetic materials and machine-cut clean lines, the better.

Larger-scale rustic touches set the tone, but smaller pieces are a great way to make your home feel authentically 'country' and authentically you. Stick to the principle of natural materials and pick out what speaks to you, whether it's functional – stacked firewood; leather-upholstered furniture; antique silver napkin rings, cutlery or utensils; handmade pottery and glassware – or purely aesthetic – old wooden chopping boards; antique leather suitcases and leather-bound books; vintage postcards, photos and recipe books; patinated fluted cake tins, or indeed anything made of aged bronze, nickel, copper and pewter; or even gardening equipment, like grain scoops and old prune-drying racks.

PART 3

LA GRANGE AUX TOURTERELLES

A CASE STUDY IN HOW TO FRENCH COUNTRY

THE BARN SITS TO ONE SIDE OF THE house, between what was formerly the *conciergerie* and the walled garden. When we bought the house, the barn (*la grange*) was still in its original state: dirt floors, rat-eaten corn cobs in the loft, piles of wood and an old beaten-up ride-on mower parked in the back corner. The barn was actually in two 'sections', with the upper barn set a foot higher than the lower barn and divided from it by a thick stone wall. Both areas had been used for air-curing tobacco (grown for personal consumption, as was common practice in the Béarn many years ago), and all the beams were studded with long lengths of wire for drying the leaves. Rumour has it that the old general who built the house in the 1850s was rather fond

of a tipple, so the barns were also used for making wine. His grapes were grown further down the lane on the sunny slopes facing the Pyrénées.

The plans, interior design, painting and project management of the barn were all done by me over the course of a year and a half while I was simultaneously photographing and writing this book. When I decided to convert the barn into a little cottage, I started to document my progress and photograph each stage. Unlike the main house, this smaller project is like a vignette, a miniature project that encompasses every room in the average home, and it creates the perfect opportunity for me to walk you through the talk of 'how to French country' in real time.

THE SALVAGED ORIGINAL ROOF TILES DISGUISE THE FACT THAT THE BARN'S ROOF WAS RECENTLY RENOVATED AND REINFORCED. EQUALLY, THE NEW DORMER WINDOWS LOOK AS IF THEY'VE ALWAYS BEEN THERE, WITH THEIR LITTLE ZINC SPIKES.

BEFORE YOU START
A RENOVATION

It seems obvious, but for each element of the build – including the fit-out, decorating and furniture – make sure you have plans drawn up, the necessary construction authorisations in place, and your budget verified with at least a few quotes from accredited and reputable artisans and builders. There's nothing worse than getting to the end of a build and having no money left for furniture or curtains (these, if made to measure with beautiful fabric, can be costly). Use a spreadsheet to keep track of budgeting and payments. If you're managing the renovation yourself, make sure you understand the sequence of trades necessary to complete any given task; this way you won't waste time (or drive your subcontractors crazy) by asking them to come and do work that they can't carry out without another trade having first completed their job.

Furniture layout

A tip regarding the layout of furniture. Once your plans have been drawn up, buy a roll of architect's tracing paper – you can find this on Amazon – and lay it over the floor plan. Secure it to the table with some masking tape or some removable adhesive (such as Blu Tack) so that it's held steady, then trace around the outlines of the rooms with a ruler. This way you will have a reference when you come to overlay your furniture plan. Next, refer to the architect's scale – this is usually in the corner of the plan and is typically 1:100; that is, 1 centimetre on the drawing would be 100 centimetres in the room. Now divide the measurements of your existing furniture pieces, or those you want to buy, by 100 to get the scale measurements for your furniture layout. For example, a standard three-seater sofa is usually somewhere between 183 and 244 centimetres wide (with a depth of approximately 56 centimetres). Let's say ours is 200 centimetres wide: that means we would represent it on the plan by drawing a line 2 centimetres long. All this is even easier if you buy a scale ruler, which will have the ratios marked for you. It's often useful to have a builder's retractable metal tape measure handy so you can convert the spaces between the furniture on your floor plan with your longer tape measure, to get a true sense of the distances in a real room.

Lay out your furniture (including rugs) on the plan in pencil, bearing in mind the flow of the room. Think about where people will enter and how much space they will have to move around in. Consider the existing spaces you are already living in and take note of how much room you need between a coffee table and the sofa, or between side tables and the entry points of the room – this way you will avoid creating 'bottlenecks' (which are especially problematic in kitchen spaces, where people tend to gather). Also think about the amount of seating you need; generally, if a house sleeps eight you'll need at least eight seats, even if these include just a simple pouf or ottoman. And don't feel you need to have all the furniture against the wall. Sofas, particularly in larger rooms, look much more welcoming if they're away from the wall, with another piece of furniture against the wall behind them or against the back of the sofa itself – for example, a table with lamps.

Once you have the measurements for all your furniture pieces and rugs, you can cut them out to scale on a separate piece of paper and move them around until you've achieved a layout you're happy with.

I find it's easier to organise all the elements if I have a folder or box for each room. Into this I put the floor plans (sometimes options for two or three plans) and my feel board notes, and then I continue to add details of the furniture, textural elements, colours, fabric samples, door hardware, lighting, artwork and so on. It's just a simple way of organising your ideas in one place – otherwise samples can tend to overrun the house.

PLANNING POWER POINTS AND PLUMBING

The furniture layout stage of your planning is the perfect time to decide where you want your lamps. Floor power points can be cleverly hidden underneath sofas, allowing you to have lamps on side tables in the middle of the room; you should do this before the slab is poured – there are no second chances! If you want surround-sound speakers, pop a few extra power points in the walls or even hide them within a bookcase; in the barn, we hid ours behind the ceiling beams above the armoire. If you want outdoor lighting (such as sensor lighting for external entrances) – or an electric gate opener, underground electric dog-fencing, a pond pump for a fountain or even a power point for outdoor equipment – then factor these in when you're planning the electrics for the interior. That way, during construction, installation holes can be drilled through external walls and wiring can be run underneath the planned location of new terrace slabs or paths without any trouble. All of this is *not* so easily done retrospectively. The same goes for plumbing: if you're planning to install a barbecue area on a terrace outside the kitchen, this is the time to consider an adjoining external sink area – in addition to uplighting for feature trees, ground lighting for paths and directional lights over outdoor tables.

LEFT: AFTERNOON LIGHT IN THE BARN KITCHEN. A BOUQUET OF ROSES ADDS A POP OF JOYOUS YELLOW AMID THE EARTHY TONES OF LINEN CURTAINS, ANTIQUE COPPER POTS AND THE CALMING PATINA OF WHITE CAESARSTONE MARBLE BENCHTOPS.

RIGHT: I ALWAYS KEEP A SINGLE BLOOM FROM THE GARDEN (OR A SPRIG OF AROMATIC FOLIAGE IN THE WINTER) IN THE KITCHEN, WHERE IT WILL MAKE ME SMILE. THE SIMPLEST OF RITUALS AND A GREAT REMINDER THAT ONE IS ENOUGH.

RIGHT: I LOVE SETTING THE TABLE. I ALWAYS TUCK A SPRIG OF HERBS INTO MY RANDOM
COLLECTION OF ANTIQUE SILVER NAPKIN RINGS – TYPICALLY ROSEMARY, THYME, LAVENDER
OR BAY. GUESTS WILL BRUISE IT A LITTLE WHEN THEY TAKE THE NAPKIN FROM ITS RING,
PROVIDING AN AROMATIC *BIENVENUE* TO THE MEAL THAT AWAITS.

Choosing a colour palette

When deciding on my colour palette, I like to start by thinking about the most dominant element in the room, or the most dominant material; for example, large expanses of glass, stone walls or plasterboard walls. When I designed the main house kitchen, the first thing I decided on was the colour of the AGA; it's a huge piece of equipment located in the centre of the room. In fact, Aggie (as she's known) is the superstar of the room, and her beautiful duck-egg blue enamel had to be the main 'voice'. When I designed the barn kitchen, I was dealing with a large open-plan area, so I needed to remain mindful that any colours I introduced via substantial feature pieces – such as the armoire – would influence the adjoining lounge area, sited at the opposite end of the shared open-plan living space.

The first thing I decided on in the barn was the colour of the Lacanche stove. I remember standing there with the Lacanche agent, who enthusiastically held up a high-octane race-car red sample, explaining with a fist-thrusting movement and a grunt that it would add real 'energy' to the room. I smiled politely. Indeed, it would have … but the colour I was looking for was something more demure, something that would complement the stones in the wall and blend in with the barn's interior. I had my sights set on adding colour to something larger: the armoire.

There were countless hues I could have chosen for the armoire, but if you're going to paint a large feature piece in an open-plan room, make sure it's a colour you adore. It needs to define you and the way you want to feel *every* day of the week. I chose Autentico Code Blue because as much as I love green … and dusty pink … and mustard yellow … this shade of blue is a colour I find both calming and grounding. It's handsome yet genteel – and most of all, it's a hue that I never tire of, no matter the season.

Once you've decided on your hero colour – or neutral, if you prefer a more muted tone – it's time to refer back to your feel board notes and decide on the other colours, patterns and textures in the room. Consider all the ways you want to feel when you enter this space, as well as how you're going to use it, and take note of the room's aspect and the availability of natural light. It really is important to be realistic at this stage. If you're a family of five like us, and you enjoy informal dining with the occasional dinner party, *don't* design a dining room for the three or four evenings a year when you're going to sit down to a formal four-course meal on elegant dining chairs at a polished antique table that's susceptible to marking by heat and liquids, surrounded by walls of a deep, intimate colour that's perfect for candlelit dinners but not for the majority of meals you'll be having there during daylight hours.

Take your colour cues from things that you love. You might have a favourite rug that you want to use because it tells a meaningful story; if so, make this your hero piece. Select a colour in the rug and be led by that – it could provide inspiration for a painted sideboard or fabric for a sofa. Or, if you have a beautiful view out the window, take your colour cues from the landscape. Once you've made your decision, order some sample pots, paint the colours onto big sheets of white cardboard and then move these around the room, noticing how the different hues alter throughout the day and how they make you *feel*, particularly as the weather changes. Darker colours will make the room seem more intimate and cosy; lighter colours will make it appear larger and will reflect more of the available light.

My palette for the barn was entirely based on the building's predominant feature: the beautiful old stone walls. I wanted to maintain a gentle, earthy palette with a splash of blue-grey that talked back to the blue-grey stones dotted throughout the walls. I teamed Autentico Code Blue with soft neutrals that reflect the neutral tones of the big limestone blocks and the lime mortar. On the kitchen joinery and French doors, I used Farrow & Ball Ammonite. For the mezzanine balustrades, skirting boards and staircase, I chose Autentico French Grey, another neutral that talks back to the stones in the walls. The tumbled travertine floor tiles from Cupastone once again mirror the creamy caramel stones in the walls, and their 'Roman' format – a mix of sizes that helps break the more modern lines of a standard repeated tile – provides a more traditional irregular pattern that reflects the rustic placement of the stones in the walls. Essentially, the ground floor – being one long, open space – has the same neutral palette as the original stone structure. (By contrast, the colours in the loft – which we'll look at in my description of Stage Two of the build – are demarcated by walls, providing more room to play with colour … albeit within my very soft Béarnaise landscape palette.)

161

LEFT: CREATING A CUSTOM COLOUR PALETTE BY MIXING MID ORANGE
WITH BLUE, THEN WITH VARIOUS SHADES OF GREY.

CENTRE: CARDBOARD AND PAPER ARE GREAT FOR CLEANING BRUSHES.
SIMPLY SWISH AWAY ANY EXCESS FROM YOUR BRUSH BEFORE WASHING. THIS KEEPS ALL
BUT THE TRULY UNAVOIDABLE TRACES OF PAINT FROM WASHING DOWN THE DRAIN.

RIGHT: THE KITCHEN ARMOIRE PAINTED IN SITU. THE ISLAND BENCH,
AWAITING ITS CAESARSTONE BENCHTOP.

STAGE ONE: THE LOCK-UP

Stage one began with the roof. The oak beams were as solid as the day they went up, but the roof battens were beginning to sag and needed to be replaced. I also wanted to create an opening for a staircase to the loft and a mezzanine above the new kitchen. The floorboards in these areas were cut, opening up the lower level to the ceiling above, creating a wonderful feeling of space as you enter. Because the loft area was originally used for storing corn and hay, the crossbeams were too low to allow sufficient head height for bedrooms. To remedy this, the roofer removed the beams and created new, higher, cross supports, gaining another 60 centimetres of head height. This allows us ample space to walk without stooping.

Rather than replace the beautiful old handmade terracotta roof tiles, I opted to reuse them, cleaning and stacking them on pallets as they came down. The broken tiles were crushed and used to make gravel paths in the *potager*. We replaced the tiles on the weather-prevailing side of the barn with new ones; these can't be seen from the house, but they still have an aged patina that blends surprisingly well. Four dormer windows (called *lucarnes* or *chien-assis* in French) were installed in the roof space facing the walled garden, to capture light and help ventilate the new rooms in the loft area. We decorated each dormer's tiny roof – as well as either end of the main barn roof – with traditional handmade zinc finials known as *épis*, and mounted a magnificent handmade zinc weathervane on one end of the barn roof. When our local zinc atelier asked me what animal I'd like to adorn the weathervane, I chose the dove – not a single day passes that I don't look out the window of the main house and see turtledoves romantically cooing to one another on the barn roof. So, from the day Jean the roofer installed our magnificent dove-crested weathervane, the barn has been known as *La Grange aux Tourterelles*: Turtledove Barn.

The dividing wall between the two barn areas was knocked out, creating a long, open space; the upper level was extended to form one long kitchen/dining area, with a small step down to a sunken lounge on the lower level. This change in level, while only slight, is a subtle but effective way of zoning an open-plan space. I intentionally chose not to have a window in the sunken lounge area,

THE BARN'S NAMESAKE, THE TURTLEDOVE-TOPPED ZINC WEATHERVANE,
HOLDS COURT WITH ITS REAL-LIFE COMPANIONS.

165

making the new fireplace the focal point and the predominant aesthetic one of cocooning comfort and cosiness.

At this point, our stonemason sandblasted all the stone walls, removing the old, flaking, fragile lime mortar, before tediously repointing each and every stone with lime mortar in the traditional method. Sandblasting is a messy process, so it's always best to do this at the very beginning. There are endless colour options for traditional lime mortar, or *enduit* as it's known in French. Finding the right colour is crucial – too white and it looks fake and modern, too yellow and it looks like lemon icing on a sponge cake. I experimented until I found the perfect shade: a grey-beige (Rénopass Chaux, colour 120 – Gris Perle) that blends beautifully with the grey, beige, brown and creamy limestone colours in the stone walls. It's the same *enduit* that we used for the stone walls of the kitchen in the main house.

Once the repointing was complete, water pipes and electrical conduit were laid within the floor foundations and the slab was poured. I've renovated many houses over the years, and every time we pour a slab, each member of the family places a coin in the concrete and makes a wish. The slabs we've poured at this house have all had the addition of a heart-shaped stone from the local river, with each of our names written on it. For some reason, the Gave d'Oloron seems to make lots of these heart-shaped rocks (my youngest, Toby, says swimming in the river washes you with love; I think he might be right).

The new opening between the two barn spaces was built using cheap red-brick blocks and a concrete beam; the blocks and the beam were then rendered with the same mortar that was used in the joints, creating a seamless flow and cleverly disguising the ugly brick and concrete beneath. The barn's original stone niches were also repointed. These traditional little openings within the wall were used by farmers as handy shelves. Nowadays, they make sweet features in barn conversions for displaying books, flowers and candles.

TOP LEFT TO BOTTOM RIGHT: BATHROOM PLUMBING CONCEALED WITHIN A RED-BRICK CAVITY, READY TO BE RENDERED IN LIME MORTAR; THE SUNKEN LOUNGE ROOM, PRE-FIREPLACE; THE KITCHEN CABINET WALLS, CONSTRUCTED FROM RED BRICK, READY TO BE RENDERED WITH LIME MORTAR; THE ATTIC, LOOKING TOWARDS WHAT WILL BE THE GREEN BEDROOM. NEW OPENINGS CUT INTO THE FLOORBOARDS FOR THE MEZZANINE BALCONY.

The barn kitchen begins

Kitchens are the heart of the home, so it's important to make this room feel as beautiful and functional as you can. Although beauty and big bucks are not always mutually exclusive, it *is* possible to create a lovely French country kitchen that's affordable – you just have to approach it a little creatively. When I designed the barn kitchen, I wanted it to feel rustic, with a budget to match. To achieve this, I reduced my joinery costs by building the main structure of the island bench and base cabinets out of red-brick blocks. These could be laid quickly – also helping to reduce the overall cost – and once up, they could be just as quickly rendered, with the same *enduit* we used for the walls.

Before the barn kitchen walls were sandblasted and repointed, I had the electrician chase-in the wall-mounted power points at benchtop height. In my kitchens I always opt for double power points, allowing for at least one or two with a USB for phone charging. I also always position a double power point at the end of any island benchtops (the side you don't have a direct view of from the dining area is best) for plugging in appliances that you don't use often, such as stick blenders or hand-held beaters. If the island bench is in the middle of the room, you can install a flush-mounted power-point tower in the benchtop itself, which pops up when you need it. Another handy country kitchen addition for the benchtop is a flush-mounted waste bin; bear in mind, though, that it will take up some of your under-bench space. In the case of the barn kitchen, there was not enough room, and so a simple benchtop compost bin suffices.

THE GOLDEN TRIANGLE

Because the kitchen in the barn was created from scratch, I had the luxury of designing it with the layout I wanted. I placed the stove against the back wall, centred on the French doors facing it, and installed the sink and taps in the island bench, centred in relation to the stove opposite. To the left of the sink, in the island base cabinets, I located the integrated dishwasher, and to the far right, under-bench fridge and freezer drawers. This layout is often described as the 'golden triangle' of fridge, sink and oven, and it allows you to function as efficiently as possible in your kitchen.

With efficiency in mind, it's important to remember that it's best to allow a minimum of 900 millimetres between an island bench and the wall cabinets – this will ensure people can move about freely without having to shuffle past one another like crabs. Also, think about your bench height. An average benchtop height is 900 millimetres, but if your family is tall it could be as high as 1050 millimetres; if you're shorter, it might be only 850 millimetres high. If in doubt, experiment. Find an old door and chock it up on two stools. Try out a variety of heights for your door 'benchtop' by putting a chopping board on the surface and cutting something up. You'll soon work out what height feels best. Although they are more expensive, I (nearly) always opt for 40-millimetre-thick benchtops; they create a more solid and luxurious feel. However, in the case of the barn kitchen I opted for a more economical 20 millimetres.

THE KITCHEN, FRESHLY RENDERED, LOOKING TOWARDS THE SUNKEN LOUNGE ROOM.

Carpentry

During stage one we treated the oak beams in the barn with an anti-termite, anti-woodborer product. France, as I discovered soon after moving here, is home to a host of destructive wood-munching beetles, including the deathwatch beetle (*Xestobium rufovillosum*), house longhorn beetle (*Hylotrupes bajulus*) and powderpost beetle (*Lyctus brunneus*). Some of these make holes 6–8 millimetres in diameter and can cause severe structural damage.

The two sets of French doors were designed to fit the original barn-door openings. They were made by André Chabalgoity (affectionately known as Dédé to family and friends – so I'm proud to know him as Dédé now, too), a local carpenter and artisan who, along with his wingman Jean-Marc Idiart, has worked with me throughout the renovation of the main house and the barn. His craftmanship is second to none, and it always comes with a great big smile and a string of jokes … he's utterly adorable.

To comply with French energy standards, the doors and dormer windows are double glazed. The French doors also have a long louvred window at the top for ventilation. The eternal question in the country is how to keep out the flies. One ingenious solution Dédé has come up with in the main house is a pull-down flyscreen, mounted outside the window on the upper sill, which clicks into a track at the base of the windowsill when down. When the flyscreen is up, it's almost invisible; when down, it's so subtle that you'd hardly know it was there. In the case of the barn, I'm waiting to see how many flies sneak in through the louvre window at the top of the doors before deciding if a flyscreen there is necessary. When it comes to questions of necessity and budget, I'm a firm advocate of the 'wait and see' approach.

PREPARING FOR THE TERRACE SLAB TO BE POURED AND EXTERIOR WALL TO BE REPOINTED WITH TRADITIONAL LIME MORTAR.

STAGE TWO: THE FIT-OUT

With the barn watertight, and secure with windows and doors – and with the bones of the kitchen built – it was time to begin the process of fitting it out. The loft area walls were the first thing on the agenda, which our beloved builder Alex threw himself into constructing in record time. Two bedrooms were created at each end of the barn, with a bathroom and separate laundry cupboard in the middle, as well as a narrow desk area in the mezzanine corridor above the kitchen. I wanted to make a feature of the beautiful oak beams in the hips at each end of the barn, so Alex expertly plastered around them, creating a small recess underneath for the bed. In the underside of the beams, I installed flush-mounted reading lights that can be switched on and off from beside the bed.

I chose to use natural marble for the windowsills inside the four dormer windows in the loft. Marble can be quite expensive, but if you only need a small amount, offcuts can be a cost-effective alternative. I sourced all the marble for the windowsills from a demolition yard – they were actually old marble counter-tops from furniture that had succumbed to rot or borer infestation. The great advantage of using salvaged pieces like this is that they have smooth pencil edges – a finished edge as opposed to rough-sawn. Once they were cut to size and placed in position, they looked like they were the originals. I paid €20 for the set of four windowsills.

Building the fireplace

While Alex built the rooms upstairs, work began on the central fireplace in the sunken lounge area. This was designed around a huge 1-tonne piece of stone bought from the derelict garden of what was once an old abbey. The foundations of the hearth were built in a combination of stone and concrete block, and then – with the help of an excavator, a tip truck, the hay-bale forks on our neighbour's huge tractor, some big pieces of metal pipe and four strong men – the huge block of stone was lifted, rolled, heaved and jacked into place. From this point on, the fireplace insert was installed by a professional company who ensured the construction and flue all met French safety standards. We used

GOODBYE LADDER! THE STAIRCASE IS INSTALLED AND THE TUMBLED TRAVERTINE MARBLE TILES ARE LAID.

173

a Cheminées Philippe insert, bought secondhand, but unused, for the bargain price of just €200. It has the advantage of being both a slow combustion heater (when the door is shut) and an open fire (when the door is lifted up into the cavity behind the chimney breast).

The wood burner is the only heating in the barn; ducting heat from the fireplace to the loft areas above helps to distribute heat more efficiently. In addition, we installed the most energy-efficient insulation available to ensure that what heat we gained from the fire wasn't lost. In rural France, we have the benefit of buying wood felled from trees in our community forests to use in our fireplaces and wood burners. These are managed for continual community use, facilitating affordable and sustainable heating … it's also good for your health, because once your reserved tree is felled, it's up to you to go into the forest to chop it up and remove it!

If you don't want a huge fireplace but still want oodles of French old-world charm, Godin's 'Petit Godin' cast-iron wood burner is a great choice. The Godin foundry has been making these charming traditional top-opening enamelled cast-iron wood stoves since 1840. Godin's blue enamel is utterly divine in a French country barn or living room.

The chimney breast itself was built using fire-rated fibre-cement board. To marry the various materials with the stone walls, the concrete block was rendered in the same Gris Perle lime mortar, and the fibre-cement sheeting was painted with lime wash paint from Bauwerk, colour Catkin. The beautiful muted patina of Bauwerk lime wash paint softens hard lines and lends a velvety softness to the surface, making it the perfect backdrop for hanging an old foxed mirror to reflect both daylight and candlelight.

Dédé made the timber mantelpiece using an ancient salvaged oak beam. The result of using old materials mixed with new materials disguised as old is both economical and seamless; the ancient hearth stone and oak mantelpiece greet the eye with a resoundingly convincing impression of times past. Allowing the newer materials to blend in with the rest of the lime-rendered walls and stone wall joints means they become blurred and invisible. The alternative, of course, was to construct a fireplace entirely out of salvaged stone, which would have more than quadrupled the price. So, in this case, a bit of (quite literal) smoke and mirrors saved the budget.

THE FIREPLACE TAKES SHAPE AND THE KITCHEN BOOKSHELVES ARE PAINTED BEFORE BEING INSTALLED.

COMPOSITE BENCHTOPS

Composite or manufactured benchtops are a great choice for French country kitchens. There a number of reputable manufacturers. Caesarstone pioneered the category of quartz stone composites thirty years ago, and another well-regarded brand is Silestone, which I used for the kitchen in the main house.

Composite benchtops come in pre-cut slabs, so if you're designing an island benchtop and want to avoid a join, make sure you design your island based on the size of the slab. A Caesarstone slab measures 3050 x 1440 millimetres.

General maintenance of composite benchtops simply involves wiping with a wet cloth. For anything a bit greasier, I use Marius Fabre savon noir spray, and if the mark is really stubborn I use a French product called Pierre d'Argent, made with white clay. It's a biodegradable, gentle abrasive that really lifts stubborn dirt and grime. I was told French housewives swear by it, and now, so do I.

Installing the barn kitchen

Stage two saw the installation of the eagerly anticipated Lacanche Cluny stove (in colour Gris-Faïence) as well as the appliances within the island bench space – the under-bench fridge and freezer drawers and an integrated dishwasher. Between them, Dédé installed a set of drawers and a sink cupboard with concealed bin; he also made integrated door fronts for the two appliances in order to create one continuous line of joinery. All the kitchen cabinetry was handmade in the traditional way using solid timber and fitted with modern soft-close mechanisms. It was then painted in Farrow & Ball Estate Eggshell for Timber, in colour Ammonite, as were the interiors of both sets of French doors and the six Thonet stools at the front of the island bench.

The base cabinets along the wall opposite the island bench were simply fitted with clear-lacquered solid-timber shelving. The lacquer makes them resistant to grease stains and general wear and tear – and therefore far more serviceable. I designed a power point in the back corner of this under-bench area for the microwave. (I loathe the look of these appliances, but admit they are handy.)

The benchtops are Caesarstone, colour Frosty Carrina, which is as close as you'll get to the look of real marble. Don't get me wrong, I adore marble – and perhaps if I lived alone, wasn't a messy cook and didn't love red wine so much, I'd happily settle for a creamy white slab of Calacatta. This is where composite quartz stone comes to the rescue.

Caesarstone is made with 93 per cent raw quartz. On the Mohs scale of mineral hardness, with 10 being a diamond and 1 being talc, quartz is 7, as is granite (6–7), whereas marble is 3; so, despite being a marble look-alike, quartz is a whole lot tougher. When it comes to spills, Caesarstone's quartz surfacing eliminates the need for frequent treatments and makes the surface resistant to stains and heat. Marble, on the other hand, is far more porous, making it especially susceptible to acids such as citrus juice and wine, which will 'etch' the marble. Anything containing beta-carotene is another marble foe.

On either side of the wall-mounted rangehood there is open shelving, made from old salvaged oak – once again, transformed into classic French country–style joinery by Dédé. Dédé also created the surround for the rangehood using an exquisitely carved piece of oak from a bed that I salvaged at a house clearance in a nearby village.

THE CAESARSTONE BENCHTOPS ARE INSTALLED.

FRENCH STOVES

So revered is the art of cooking here in France that a stove is referred to as a *piano*. The Lacanche Cluny in the barn comes with 250 years of French expertise. Lacanche stoves are handcrafted in Burgundy, using porcelain enamel, stainless steel and cast-iron. They are also made to order with customised colour, finish and configuration. Upon ordering a magnificent *piano* on which to compose gastronomic symphonies, the sense of anticipation experienced feels a bit like awaiting the arrival of a brand-new baby. I've called my handsome silver fox George (after George Clooney).

Another iconic French stove is La Cornue. If Lacanche is the Rolls Royce of French stoves, then this brand is the Aston Martin. These *pianos* are manufactured not only to order but also by hand; specifically, the hands of one individual artisan, known as a *compagnon*, whose artisan's number is recorded on each *piano* that they produce. The entry-level CornuFé model starts at just over €5600 – which might explain why the rest are 'Price on demand'.

Wall shelving

I *love* books, and a kitchen without books, in my opinion, is just not a kitchen. I have therefore dedicated an entire wall to my vast cookbook and garden library. It allows me easy access and sits alongside the huge refectory table in the dining area. This way, when I'm taking a break, I can just reach for the shelf and sit with a cup of tea in the sunlight, indulging in my greatest pleasure: turning pages. Books add unique colour, pattern and a sense of rhythm to an interior palette, so you should also consider them as part of the decorative elements in a room. The shelves are made from cheap pine and are painted in Farrow & Ball Ammonite, which ties in with the kitchen cabinetry. I installed a concealed power point behind the bookshelf for a lamp, as well as adjustable shelves to accommodate different-sized stacking options and decorative elements like vases of fresh flowers.

The staircase

Finally, the day arrived for the beautiful staircase to be installed. We'd been using a ladder to gain access to the loft, so this day couldn't have come soon enough, particularly for someone like me who's terrified of heights. I designed the balustrades based on the patterns of those found on traditional Béarnaise verandahs and simply gave a drawing to Dédé, who magically turned it into the basis for the most beautiful flowing staircase and a balustrade for the mezzanine. These I painted in Autentico Vintage chalk-based paint in French Grey.

The floors

The concrete floors were all overlaid with tumbled travertine marble from Cupastone. This is the same stone we used for the kitchen and snug room floors in the main house, as well as for all the outdoor paving around the pool. Having lived with it for more than five years, I can safely say it's the best floor surface for a family of five and two dogs living in the countryside. The tumbled patina and natural colour variations of the travertine marble are incredibly forgiving when it comes to the dirt and mud that's inevitably walked in from the fields and the garden. The stones were joined with a beige grout, and Cupastone's matt sealant was applied to the surface. Their cream-and-honey-coloured palette beautifully complements the colours of the stone walls, and their irregular surface is just the perfect amount of rustic; anything more would be too much, anything too smooth would look too modern. What's more, they're reasonably priced compared with salvaged flagstones, which would also be ideal but were outside my budget – by a long way!

An armoire

To save further joinery costs, I bought an old armoire from a charity shop for €150 and painted it with Autentico Vintage chalk-based paint in Code Blue, using Autentico Vintage in colour Brut on the central backboard to break up the colour a little. I then finished it with clear wax. Buying a piece of furniture and repainting it in a colour that will make you feel great is much cheaper than installing cabinetry – and often gives you far more storage space anyway. Old pieces of furniture are also inevitably better made than cheap MDF flat-pack cabinetry. I used leftover wallpaper offcuts from the main house to line the insides of the armoire doors, which is a lovely way to give yourself a little bit of unexpected colour and pattern each time you open the pantry.

If you don't have wallpaper offcuts and really want something special, you can also use beautiful block-printed French domino paper from Parisian paper specialists Antoinette Poisson (see page 135). Their range of gorgeous 18th century–inspired domino papers make the most exquisite lining for the insides of cupboard doors; they can even be displayed in a frame on the wall – they're true works of art in themselves.

Another idea for wallpapering the inside of armoire doors could be to decoupage using pages from old French recipe books found at charity shops. Use your imagination! Another very 'French country' armoire tip is to line the shelves with paper and simply secure with thumb tacks. This very practical tradition helps keep shelves clean; I also sprinkle my lining paper with a few drops of French lavender or peppermint oil to keep the pantry moths at bay. When the paper gets too dirty, simply replace it.

WALLPAPER REMNANTS ARE USED TO PAPER THE INSIDE OF THE ARMOIRE DOORS.

Dining room furniture

I really wanted an old French refectory or farmhouse table for the barn. One day, when I was passing a Basque woodworker's atelier, I popped in and inquired if they had any antiques. They apologised and said no, but as I was on my way out the door the owner called me back, asking if I'd like to see something he'd had sitting in his back shed for years. It was perfect; not quite an antique, but beautifully handcrafted. The only problem was that it weighed a tonne, literally. We struck a bargain, which included delivery, and a few days later it arrived – carried in by four huge Basque men, red-faced, muscles straining. I think it's safe to say, the table will never again leave the room, so I'm glad I like it. I painted the base with Autentico Vintage chalk-based paint in Brut and left the timber top natural, except for an extra layer of protection using Autentico Grandiose Hardwax Oil in Natural (clear finish). If you don't have the budget for an old table, find one within your price range that has the same look as a traditional farmhouse table (pine stores often sell these) and simply paint the base with chalk-based paint – a darker hue or grey is best. This will instantly transform it into something much more French country. If the top is not a particularly nice wood, you could try staining it. Autentico Grandiose Hardwax Oil also comes in a range of tints that can give the wood a subtle, vintage, country-style patina. Alternatively, an old/dark oak stain could be a good choice if you're after something darker to disguise a more orange-tinged timber.

Cross-back bistro chairs were my choice for the barn; I bought these new from Bertrand Souviron at Souviron Palas in Oloron-Sainte-Marie. This charming French mini department store sells everything from elegant French pyjamas in old-fashioned boxes to the bed, sofa and chairs I bought for the barn. Bertrand and his seamstress also made all our curtains, as well as those in the barn's bedrooms and kitchen. He is the fourteenth generation in his family to run this beautiful historic shop overlooking the Gave d'Oloron.

THE ULTIMATE FRENCH COUNTRY DINING CHAIR

I think French country kitchens are always best with wooden benches, French bistro chairs or a collection of random farmhouse-style wooden chairs (painted or natural). That said, I used modern design classics in the main kitchen: one of my favourite iconic chair designs for each member of the family, matched to their personality – Toby's is Philippe Starck's 'Mr. Impossible'! My chairs are all white, but if you love colour, it can be another great way to celebrate each family member's personality; it's also a fun way of adding multiple colours to a neutral interior.

When it comes to French bistro chairs, the original French brands are Baumann, Martin Méallet, Thonet and Chez Kohn. If you're lucky, you can still find antique sets of these chairs online via Selency, eBay or at brocantes.

I have a set of antique Thonet bentwood chairs around the dining room table in the main house, which I've collected individually over the years. They truly are the ultimate little black dress of the chair world, just as happy in a modern city loft as they are in a farmhouse. I give mine an annual glue and screw tightening as they can become a bit loose, but apart from that they're extremely easy to maintain.

Woven Parisian outdoor chairs are another great option. Maison Gatti and Maison Louis Drucker are two of the original manufacturers still in production today. These chairs are also a super choice for introducing colour and woven texture to the dining area if your room is predominantly neutral and needs a pop of French pattern and colour.

The barn bathroom

For the tiles in the bathroom upstairs, I chose a design by Caroline Diaz and Céline Héno, from French design house Mini Labo for Maison Bahya, called Camelia, in colour Vieux Rose ('Old Pink'). These beautiful Moroccan-manufactured cement tiles are like a floor rug for the bathroom, adorning it with pattern and creating a feeling of intimacy that's often lacking in this space.

On the walls I used handmade rectangular Bahya zellige tiles. The rich burgundy colour was my own little homage to one of my favourite things, red wine, but it also speaks to the origins of the barn as a little winery. These tiles, teamed with the deep dusty pink/brown of Autentico Versante Matt (Autentico's washable bathroom paint), colour Bari, make for an atmosphere that feels cocooning as soon as you enter; a place where you can lie back in the bath surrounded by candles and completely unwind. Poor Alex graciously undertook the tedious job of laying the delicate zellige wall tiles in a chevron pattern – and promptly announced when he was finished that it was his first and last foray with zellige in this format. Zellige tiles are handmade from terracotta, as well as being hand-glazed, and are extremely fragile when being cut. The results, though, are exquisite, reminding me of all the beautiful *hammam*s I've visited in Morocco over the years. If you'd like to try them yourself, make sure you allow for a little more than the usual 10 per cent wastage.

The shower/bath wet room was finished in tadelakt lime plaster. My love of tadelakt began with my first trip to Morocco and has grown with each subsequent visit. If you've ever been to a *hammam*, chances are you've experienced tadelakt lime plaster's impressive waterproofing capabilities and seen the way it can be formed into a continuous, seamless surface. This makes it a great choice for bathrooms, because there are no joins – the plaster surface simply flows around corners and up and along ceilings. We had the plaster colour-matched to Autentico Versante Matt, colour Bari.

The sliding bathroom door was once a shutter from the internal verandah of the main house. I left it sitting propped up against a wall in the garden for more than three years before I asked Dédé if he could convert it into a sliding barn-style door. In his usual jovial way, he responded with a resounding '*Mais oui, Sara!*' A sliding door is a great way to maximise space in tight areas, like hallways, that don't allow for a door to swing. The beautiful weathered oak is also a lovely rustic feature alongside the wallpapered walls, and the barn-style door mechanism is a nice reference to the original function of the building. (The barn's blue bedroom also features a sliding door. I disguised its exposed silver mechanism with a custom-designed wooden sconce, a tiny detail that evokes the craftsmanship of French country homes – another little Dédé masterpiece.)

The vanity for the bathroom I found at a local *brocante* and painted with Autentico Vintage chalk-based paint using a colour I made myself: a combination of the colours Pebbles and Dolphin. It was formerly a small marble-topped commode, but with Alex's ever-steady hands, a hole was cut in the fragile old marble top and an undermount sink installed, along with a set of vintage-style taps. Dédé's assistant, Jean-Marc, then cut the drawer faces away from the carcass and mounted them as false fronts. The carpenters also made a new shelf inside the vanity to accommodate the waste pipes and maximise storage space.

TOP LEFT: RUNNING ON A SLIDING RAIL, THE BATHROOM DOOR WAS ORIGINALLY AN OLD SHUTTER FROM THE MAIN HOUSE THAT SAT OUTSIDE FOR ALMOST FOUR YEARS BEFORE I HAD A LITTLE BRAINWAVE AND REINSTATED IT HERE.

TOP RIGHT: THERE'S SOMETHING ABOUT THE COMBINATION OF LAMPLIGHT AND REPURPOSED FURNITURE IN A BATHROOM – ANY TRACE OF THE CLINICAL IS REPLACED WITH A FEELING OF COSY CONTENTMENT, PARTICULARLY WHEN PAIRED WITH THE BURGUNDY-HUED TILES SEEN BOTTOM LEFT.

Wallpapering the bedrooms and hallway

I had such a lot of fun indulging my love of surface design in the barn. The loft bedrooms are true barn-style rooms, with their sloping walls and little dormer windows, and I wanted to create a feeling of being wrapped up in one of granny's old eiderdown quilts. Because I'd used dusty pink and deep burgundy in the bathroom, I wanted to stick to the calming hues of green and blue for the bedrooms. One good trick for using wallpapers in adjoining areas is to select two designs from the same collection or design house. In the case of the mezzanine/hallway and one of the bedrooms, I chose two from Sandberg Wallpaper. They share the same base of colours, but are differentiated by their design; their common Sandberg heritage has the subtle effect of tricking the eye, lending them an almost indefinable compatibility. For the bedroom, I chose a beautiful Sandberg Wallpaper by Sara Bergqvist, called Karolina Blue. Its delicate little bay leaf design reminds me of summer afternoons spent lying on the lawn in the walled garden adjoining the barn, looking up at the canopy of the trees that overhang the garden. It's also a smaller pattern, which doesn't overwhelm the small space, and at the same time makes it feel like the kind of room Goldilocks might snuggle down in after a warm bowl of porridge. Bay leaves symbolise wisdom, prosperity and honour, and were a popular motif in the Swedish Gustavian period.

For the hallway, I chose a design by Karolina Kroon for Sandberg Wallpaper, called Karl Blue. This classic 18th century–inspired design features a little olive wreath. The ancient Greeks and Romans believed olive branches symbolised strength, wealth and stability, something you can never have enough of these days, so it was a firm favourite from the outset.

For the bedroom at the other end of the loft, I went for something a little more animated, indulging my obsession with birds. I chose a Boråstapeter Chinoiseries design by Sissa Sundling, called Paradise Birds. The combination of the loft roofline and the design makes you feel like you've just entered an enchanted forest. The soft sage green casts a calming spell that rendered even my rather doubtful and macho wallpaperer virtually speechless when it was finished; he simply nodded and shrugged his shoulders, saying with a little smile, 'C'est vrais Sara, il est beau.'

TOP LEFT TO BOTTOM RIGHT: A ROLL OF SANDBERG CARL BLUE WALLPAPER (USED IN THE HALLWAY) WITH WALLPAPERING TOOLS; THE WALLPAPER IN PLACE, ADORNED WITH TWO ANTIQUE PRINTS OF TURTLEDOVES BOUGHT ON ETSY. NEVER BE AFRAID TO HANG ART ON PAPERED WALLS. THE LAYERING OF PATTERN IS KEY TO ITS CHARM; THE BACK WALL OF THE DRESSING AREA WAS PAINTED WITH LEFTOVER AUTENTICO CHALK PAINT IN CODE BLUE, ITS DEEP TONE GIVING THE ROOM A GREATER SENSE OF DEPTH. THE SPACE WAS FITTED OUT WITH A MIXTURE OF AFFORDABLE FLAT-PACK WARDROBE UNITS AND STANDARD RODS AND SHELVING, WHICH ALEX CLEVERLY CUSTOM-FITTED FOR A FRACTION OF THE PRICE NORMALLY PAID FOR MADE-TO-MEASURE WARDROBE UNITS; THE MEZZANINE HALLWAY ABOVE THE KITCHEN LEADS THROUGH TO THE GREEN BEDROOM.

LEFT: HERE IN THE BARN'S BLUE BEDROOM, THE CANOPY OF FOLIAGE CREATED BY SANDBERG'S KAROLINA PATTERN MAKES IT FEEL LIKE YOU'RE SLEEPING IN A TREEHOUSE. IT SMELLS AMAZING TOO, WITH A MELANGE OF COMFORTING EARTHY AROMAS: BEESWAX ON OLD OAK, SISAL RUGS, FRESHLY LAUNDERED LINEN SHEETS DRIED IN THE SUNSHINE.

CENTRE: THESE OIL PAINTINGS FORM PART OF A GALLERY WALL I ARRANGED IN THE STAIRWELL. THEY WERE BOUGHT AT *VIDE GRENIERS* AND *BROCANTES* FOR AS LITTLE AS €5 EACH. THE HANDCARVED WOODEN CLOGS ARE ANTIQUE BÉARNAISE, A STYLE HISTORICALLY WORN BY FARMERS.

188

RIGHT: THE GREEN BEDROOM. THE SIMPLE IKEA SEAGRASS RUG OFFSETS THE ANTIQUE BED BOUGHT FROM AN OLD HOUSE NEARBY. TWO BOTANICAL PRINTS, BOUGHT FOR ME BY ANNABELLE FROM PORTOBELLO MARKET IN LONDON, HANG IN FRAMES PAINTED IN LEFTOVER CHALK PAINT FROM SAMPLE POTS. MISMATCHED BEDSIDE TABLES ARE UNITED WITH THE SAME AUTENTICO CHALK PAINT. BEDLINEN IS ORGANIC HEMP FROM COULEUR CHANVRE IN SAINT-JEAN-DE-LUZ, ACCENTED WITH CAÏ FAHREL WOODBLOCK PRINT CUSHIONS.

Lighting the barn

The barn's windows and doors face south-east, flooding the rooms with natural light that softens rather than bounces when it hits the stone walls and floor. To highlight the stone, I have used commercial LED strip lighting, which is concealed on the inside of the beams closest to the walls, subtly washing them with warm light.

There are four feature pendant lights downstairs – one with a woven shade (made by a women's cooperative in Burkina Faso and purchased from a local design store in Pau, called Cozyn) in the sunken lounge and a series of three fluted antique milk-glass pendants (found on Etsy) above the island bench in the kitchen. The remainder of the lighting on the ground floor is muted lamplight, with candlelight used exclusively for the dining table; I'm a great believer in meals beginning with the ceremony of striking a match.

Upstairs there are short ceiling-mounted enamel pendant lights in the bedrooms, and standard downlights with directional globes to maximise the feeling of height in what could otherwise feel like a tight loft roof space. Directional reading lights were hidden behind the beams above the beds, but small bedside lamps offer a softer alternative in the event of nocturnal bathroom visits.

Almost all the lamps upstairs and downstairs were salvaged from junk yards or bought at *brocantes* (this is a great way to save money, as lamps can be very expensive) – or found in the attic of the chateau. I used the very talented Valérie Duperray, from Abat-Jour Etc. in Orthez, to refurbish and re-cover the lampshades in the traditional artisanal French method; for the large lamp under the stairs, I chose a beautiful fabric from Clarke & Clarke called Sissinghurst Midnight/Spice, with a stunning trim from Fringe Market called Bazaar 1.5 inch Cut Fringe, in colour Chambray.

I often find lovely lamps that have been rendered outdated by bright gold bases or ugly wooden ones. I use chalk paint from sample tins to transform them, instantly erasing their dated 'Austin Powers' bravado and bringing them back to a softer country hue and flat paint finish.

THE SUNKEN LOUNGE, TILED WITH CUPASTONE. THE ANTIQUE RUG WAS BOUGHT AT A *BROCANTE*, AS WERE THE TWO SINGLE CHAIRS AND TWO THATCHED STOOLS (GREAT AS SIDE TABLES, OR AS EXTRA SEATING WHEN THERE'S A CROWD). THE MUCH-LOVED WHITE TABLE (BACK RIGHT), MADE BY JO VINKS USING PAINTED EUCALYPTUS STICKS, WAS AMONG THE FEW PERSONAL ITEMS I KEPT AND SHIPPED OVER FROM AUSTRALIA.

191

STAGE THREE:
THE END IS JUST THE
BEGINNING

To say the barn is complete would be untrue. Authentic interiors take time; there's no silver bullet and nor should there be. Just as we grow and evolve over time as individuals, so too should our homes. If you finish a project with every piece in place, I think you have to question if those details are really authentic or if they're just there to fill a void. Budgets don't always stretch to cover our every whim and desire, and this isn't a failure on our part, it's simply reality. We need to learn to hold back and be patient – there *should* be gaps.

For this reason, there's space for a floor lamp in the lounge, there is room left on the bookshelves for more books, there's a spot at the end of the bed in the green bedroom for a beautiful upholstered antique-fringed ottoman … and the chimney breast above the fire is empty. I've seen numerous old mirrors and paintings that could hang there. But I know that one day we'll be out at lunch with friends and, after a wonderful fire-roasted chicken and a bottle or three of Bordeaux in a charming little *auberge* somewhere, we'll stumble across an equally charming *brocante* and there it – or any of these missing pieces – will be. And it will be more than just a mirror or a painting or an ottoman: it will resonate with the thrill of discovery, with the wait that led up to finding it, and with the memory of a day, *that day*, spent with good friends, good food and the good fortune of making memories acquiring treasures with meaning and provenance.

LATE AFTERNOON. THE BARN KITCHEN, COMPLETE AND IN OPERATION.

LEFT: THE SUNKEN LOUNGE. LINEN SOFA BY LOAF UK, SHOWCASING AN ASSORTMENT OF CUSHIONS – CAÏ FAHREL WOODBLOCKS, PLAINS FROM COULEUR CHANVRE AND A FEW STRAYS MADE FROM LEFTOVER LINEN USED FOR THE KITCHEN CURTAINS. THE COFFEE TABLE WAS MADE TO MEASURE USING RECLAIMED OAK BY DÉDÉ. ON TOP OF IT IS AN ANTIQUE FRENCH PRUNE DRYING RACK, BOUGHT FROM BERGAMOTE DÉCORATION, PAU. I LOVE TO LAYER TABLETOPS WITH TRAYS AND BOXES – THEY ADD INTEREST, FRAME WHATEVER YOU DRESS THE TABLETOP WITH AND SOFTEN LARGE, SOLID SURFACES.

CENTRE: I LOVE A GOOD DRINKS TROLLEY FOR A DIGESTIF AFTER DINNER. THIS ONE HAS AN ANTIQUE CRYSTAL ICE BUCKET (BOUGHT FOR JUST €8), A RANDOM COLLECTION OF CRYSTAL GLASSES WE WERE GIVEN AS WEDDING PRESENTS (AND ACTUALLY USE!) AND A SMALL CIGAR HUMIDOR BELOW. JUST ADD SULTRY JAZZ, A WHIFF OF CIGAR SMOKE, A COSY FIRE ... AND LISTEN TO THE ICE CUBES TINKLE IN YOUR GLASS!

PART 4

LIVING WITH
THE SEASONS

THE FRENCH COUNTRY KITCHEN

AT THE HEART OF ANY FRENCH COUNTRY home is *la cuisine*, the kitchen. Preparing a regional, seasonal meal in a French country kitchen is really not so different from curating a French country interior. It draws on the same principles of authenticity and the same cues from the local landscape. It involves sourcing sustainable ingredients and instinctively mixing and adjusting them into something balanced and true.

I am always amazed that the kitchens of French houses are so small, given the country's love of food and cooking, but in reality this speaks to the simplicity of using fresh ingredients that are bought or harvested as they are needed; there's really no need for vast kitchens with big American-style fridges and unlimited storage. Although your local climate is obviously a consideration, for one of the best indications that your French country lifestyle has

spilled over onto your plate, take a look at your kitchen benchtops and cupboards: bowls, baskets and shelves – rather than your fridge – will be providing storage for much of your produce.

Harvesting from a *potager* and shopping seasonally at local farmers' markets is the antithesis of bringing home a bootload of heavy bags from the supermarket once a week. In rural France, sourcing produce is something that happens daily, and a single basket or a garden trug is generally sufficient to contain the ingredients within. Once unpacked and washed of their soil – and in my case, shelved on the butler's pantry windowsill for later use – their seasonal colour becomes vividly apparent.

A French country lifestyle is a convergence of seasons, food, artisans and traditions. This cyclical rhythm dictates how seasonal food is prepared in

---

COPPER POTS ON THE AGA WITH A PLAIT OF GARLIC.

the kitchen. When there's a season of plenty, we preserve and pickle and prepare confit. When the days are short, we reach into our pantries for the bounty of the previous season's harvest: for nuts and jams, pickles and pâtés, or for nourishing jars of *piperade*, a local tomato and pepper sauce. Tender spring vegetables need no more than a very quick steam or sauté to lock in their delicate flavour. In the heat of summer, when appetites need a little coaxing, vegetables are often better eaten raw as crudités or in salads. As the temperature drops, root vegetables roasted in seasoned duck fat reserved from *confit* duck legs provide that delicious crispy crunch so synonymous with cold-climate comfort food. Regional French food doesn't try too hard because it doesn't need to; it honours the ingredients, and when the season for that ingredient has finished, it moves onto another. It doesn't try to be what it's not.

In my time here in the Béarn, I have learned that if you immerse yourself in the traditional pursuits of procuring local ingredients, whether that be by fishing, foraging or farming, adventure will follow, leading you to the top of mountains, along riverbanks and deep into the forest. These activities reveal the way in which the food from one season influences the traditions and lifestyle of another. Come spring, as you are hiking in the mountains, you might take a portable snack of *saucisson* that a local farmer made in winter; in autumn, you may eat it as part of a picnic while foraging for *morilles* (morels) and wild *ail des ours* (literally, 'bear's garlic').

When we allow ourselves to respond to the seasons, we instinctively furnish our plates with what our bodies need, rather than the commercial 'solutions' to things we don't: the fast, the convenient and the ever-available, the empty calories of processed foods that may have been shipped from the other side of the world. And we reduce our carbon footprint. Our food choices represent a powerful way to make a positive impact on climate change. The French countryside is unbelievably beautiful, but if we don't all support the logic of eating our view and supporting sustainable local farmers, it simply won't always look the way it does now.

Curating a sustainably sourced seasonal meal is an act of love, for the planet, your community, yourself and your family. Like a beautiful home, seasonal meals are all about the way they make you feel; thoughtfully considered creations that evoke joy and wellbeing, set on a simple plate at a beautifully laid table in the seasonal theatre that is *la cuisine*.

THE WEDNESDAY MARKET IN NAVARRENX, THE 16TH-CENTURY CHURCH OF SAINT-GERMAIN D'AUXERRE IN THE BACKGROUND. LOUIS XIII ONCE ATTENDED MASS HERE.

La cuisine d'été

THE SUMMER KITCHEN

SUMMER IS THE SEASON WHEN APPETITES often need to be enticed – when the heat becomes oppressive, a simple garden salad is all that's required. This is the time when the jam pan is on the stove, dealing with the surplus of berries, peaches and plums. It's also when we spend hot summer evenings down by the river, often with what's known in France as an *apéro dînatoire*: a collection of small dishes, food that can be slowly grazed on rather than eaten all at once. Summer is the time for harvesting lemon verbena and linden flowers to make refreshing jugs of iced tea with slices of fresh lemon, and for homemade peach wine.

The summer harvest includes

Basque peppers – *piments Basque*

blackberries – *mûres*

blueberries – *myrtilles*

corn – *maïs*

cucumbers – *concombres*

eggplant – *aubergine*

figs – *figues*

fresh herbs – *herbes fraîches*

garlic – *ail*

grapes – *raisins*

green beans – *haricots verts*

melons – *melons*

nectarines – *nectarines*

onions – *oignons*

peaches – *pêches*

plums – *prunes*

potatoes – *pommes de terre*

raspberries – *framboises*

summer lettuce – *laitue d'été*

summer squash – *potimarron*

tomatoes – *tomates*

zucchini – *courgettes*

SUMMER BERRIES WITH WHIPPED CREAM ATOP A MUCH-LOVED HANDPAINTED TRAY,
BOUGHT WHILE WE LIVED IN RUSSIA.

Oeufs d'été
SUMMER EGGS

This very simple breakfast could be served any time of year, but I call it 'summer eggs' because it's something we love to eat when the sun rises early and we can enjoy breakfast on the kitchen terrace. In a small saucepan, make a *beurre noisette* by heating some unsalted butter until it foams and forms little brown specks at the bottom of the pan. Remove from the heat, whisk in a teaspoon of powdered *piment Béarnais* (or a *mild* chilli powder) and set aside somewhere warm. In another small saucepan, add 1 cup of organic sheep's milk yoghurt, a squeeze of lemon juice and a little crushed garlic. Warm slightly and set aside. Place a frypan over medium heat and add a little canola oil and 1–2 teaspoons of whole coriander seeds, toasting until fragrant. Crack two eggs into the pan and fry (to ensure the yolks are still runny, place a lid over the pan to steam the eggs). When the eggs are cooked, top with the reserved warm sheep's milk yoghurt and drizzle over the *beurre noisette*. Scatter with *fleur de sel* (or another quality salt) and some chilli flakes. Serve with buttered toasted baguette.

PIPERADE

This is a Basque sauce (known in the Basque language, Euskera, as *pipperada*), but as we live on the border of the Pays Basque and the Béarn I think I can be excused for including it. Almost every local I know grows the ingredients in their garden and makes this sauce throughout the summer. It's incredibly simple, and can be used to accompany a grilled tuna steak or braised chicken pieces.

SERVES 4

1 kg organic cooking tomatoes

3 tablespoons mildly flavoured olive oil (not extra virgin)

2 onions, diced

6–8 small green Paprika Anglet peppers (or 1 green capsicum), seeded and thinly sliced into long strips

2–4 Espelette peppers (or 2 red capsicums), seeded and thinly sliced into long strips

1–3 garlic cloves, finely sliced

1 bay leaf (fresh or dry, but I prefer fresh)

Score the tops of the tomatoes. Put into a pot of boiling water for 30 seconds, then quickly remove. Peel off the skin, then halve the tomatoes and remove the seeds before cutting into a medium dice. Add the oil to a pan over medium heat. When the oil is hot, add the onions and sauté for 3–4 minutes, or until soft. Add the peppers and sliced garlic to the onions in the pan and continue cooking for 7 minutes, or until soft. Add the bay leaf and the tomatoes, bring the mixture to the boil, then reduce the heat and simmer until the sauce has thickened. Adjust the seasoning and use immediately.

Variation: At the end of the cooking process, whisk three to four eggs and stir through the hot sauce until the egg is set. *Piperade* with egg is often served with slices of *jambon de Bayonne*.

HOMEGROWN TOMATOES, BASQUE PEPPERS AND MELON, A GIFT FROM MY NEIGHBOUR JOJO.
OVERLEAF: BAGUETTES WERE BORN FOR SOAKING UP THE FLAVOURS OF SUMMER, SUCH AS IN THIS SIMPLE PLATTER OF ROASTED VINE TOMATOES WITH HARICOTS MAÏS DE BÉARN (YOU CAN USE CANNELLINI BEANS) BATHED IN A GARLIC, MISO AND MINT DRESSING.

Soupe de pêches Roussanne
ROUSSANNE PEACH SOUP

Recipe courtesy of Jean-Luc Vicassiau, l'Auberge de la Fontaine, Laàs

Jean-Luc Vicassiau and his wife Suzy are dear friends who run our local *auberge* in Laàs. It's a place where we spend long summer evenings on the terrace enjoying platters of *fruits de mer* with aïoli, or grilled fish with cockles and roast potatoes. The delicious seasonal offerings are impossible to choose from – but, come summer, Suzy never asks what I'll have for dessert. It's always *soupe de pêches Roussanne*, made from an ancient variety of Béarnaise peach – intensely sweet, and so fragile that it's available for just a few short weeks. Jean-Luc has kindly passed on his recipe for this classic Béarnaise dessert soup, with his very own special touch. This recipe is based on one peach per person and makes an *auberge*-sized (i.e. *large*) quantity; adjust the amounts as you require.

SERVES 10

250 g caster sugar

1 lime or ½ orange (optional)

10 freestone peaches

½ teaspoon agar-agar powder

fresh mint, whole or roughly chopped, for garnishing

Place the sugar and 1 cup of water in a pot over medium heat and stir until it comes to the boil. Boil without stirring until it thickens (it should be reduced by about a third). To flavour the syrup, you can add either the lime juice and zest, or the juice of the orange (if using the orange, pop the skin into the pot along with the juice). Remove the pot from the heat and set aside for 1 hour to infuse.

Meanwhile, fill a pot (large enough to hold the peaches) with water and bring to the boil. Carefully lower the peaches into the boiling water and leave for up to 5 minutes, or until the skin has started to loosen. Remove the peaches from the water with a slotted spoon, allow them to cool slightly and then peel away the skin. Once peeled, de-stone and cut the peaches into quarters. Bring the syrup to the boil, removing the orange peel if using. Add the agar-agar, stirring to mix through, then simmer for 2 minutes, stirring constantly. Add the peaches and simmer for another 2 minutes, or until the peaches have softened. Cool before serving.

Divide the fruit and syrup between ten bowls and top with the mint. Jean-Luc serves this with a scoop of his signature lemon verbena sorbet.

Pêches blanches à la Anne
WHITE PEACHES À LA ANNE

This recipe comes from my talented friend Anne, who grew up in Paris and studied Art History at the Sorbonne. She spent her summers in the beachside village of Hossegor in Les Landes, just an hour from us in the Béarn. Anne still holidays there to this day. One summer, when we were together in her kitchen at Hossegor, she showed me how to make this very simple dessert from her childhood. It might not even sound like a recipe, but, trust me, there is some kind of alchemy going on between the sun-ripened white peaches, red wine and fine caster sugar that creates one of the most memorable summer desserts I've ever tasted.

Take as many sun-ripened organic white peaches as you have people to feed – make sure the peaches are at room temperature so their perfume is at its most heady. If they are particularly large, one between two people will suffice. Cut the peaches into small dice and place into a *coupe à glace* (these are the lovely French glass bowls used to serve ice-cream, but any elegant dessert bowl will do). Sprinkle evenly with a little fine caster sugar and pour over enough red wine to cover while still leaving the top of the fruit exposed. Anne uses Bordeaux, which is local to our department of the Aquitaine, but you could use pinot noir or any light and fruity red wine – heavy wines will be too tannic.

OVERLEAF: THE ESTIVE, VALLÉE DE BARÉTOUS.

THE *TRANSHUMANCE* AND THE *ESTIVE*

Summer is the season of the *transhumance*, when bees, sheep, goats, cows and horses are taken up to graze on the sweet pastures of the Pyrénées after the snow melt – usually at the end of May or in early June. Shepherds live with their sheep for the duration of the summer, basing themselves in stone huts, where they milk their flocks daily. There are only three breeds permitted for making the local AOC (*appellation d'origine contrôlée*) Ossau-Iraty Brebis cheese: the Manech Tête Noire, the Manech Tête Rousse and the Basco-Béarnaise.

Late summer through to early autumn sees the return of the livestock from the mountains in the tradition of the *estive*. As they do during the *transhumance*, locals join the shepherds on the long walk, this time accompanying them home with their ewes to their farmhouses in the valley – often with the reward of a delicious communal meal when the journey is complete. The first time I joined the *estive*, I thought it would be a leisurely downhill stroll with the ewes. It's nothing of the sort. These ladies set off at a sprint in a breakneck woolly stampede that involves almost as much uphill as down.

La cuisine d'automne

THE AUTUMN KITCHEN

IF I HAD TO NOMINATE ONE SEASON AS a favourite, I think autumn would be it. The weather is at its absolute best in the Béarn at this time of year. Thanks to fairly reliable Indian summers – *les étés indiens* – outdoor dining continues throughout the season, often right up until Christmas if we're lucky. This is the time of *la chasse*, the hunting season, when camo-clad, commando-inspired hunters with brass horns and rifles prowl the forests and even the sides of roads in search of wild boar, ground birds and deer, or perch in towers high up in the trees hunting *palombe* (wild pigeon). The non-hunters like me, on the other hand, transform into neon beacons, donning bright jackets and attaching orange collars with special little brass bells to their dogs in the hope that this might make them stand out from the forest *and* the trees.

These rather high-adrenaline walks often involve mushroom foraging – and collecting basketfuls of the chestnuts that line the tracks and the forest floor with their spiky pods.

The autumn harvest includes

apples – *pommes*

beets – *betteraves*

broccoli – *brocoli*

Brussel sprouts – *choux de Bruxelles*

cabbage – *chou*

capsicums – *poivrons*

celeriac – *céleri-rave*

celery – *céleri*

chard – *bette*

chestnuts – *châtaignes*

endive – *endive*

fennel – *fenouil*

figs – *figues*

garlic – *ail*

grapes – *raisins*

green tomatoes – *tomates vertes*

hazelnuts – *noisettes*

kale – *chou kale*

kiwifruit – *kiwi*

leeks – *poireaux*

mirabelle plums – *mirabelles*

mushrooms – *champignons*

parsnips – *panais*

pears – *poires*

persimmons – *kakis*

plums – *prunes*

pumpkins – *potirons*

radishes – *radis*

rocket – *roquette*

shallots – *échalotes*

shelling beans – *haricots*

turnips – *navets*

walnuts – *noix*

winter squash – *courge d'hiver*

THE BUTLER'S PANTRY WINDOW, HOME TO A GLUT OF HOMEGROWN PUMPKINS.

217

Raisins épicés marinés au Jurançon
SPICED GRAPES IN JURANÇON

This recipe is inspired by American food writer Judy Rodgers's recipe for spiced Zante grapes. My spiced grapes are wonderful served with slow-roasted shoulder of pork, autumnal game birds or alongside pâté and charcuterie. When I help with the grape harvest (*la vendange*), I politely ask to take a few bunches of the very sweet local Petit or Gros Manseng grapes home with me, but you could use any sweet heirloom grape; the commonly available Red Flame or Thompson's Seedless would work equally well.

Wash and dry 500 grams of grapes and cut them into small clusters, removing any bruised or mouldy grapes. Place the grapes in sterilised preserving jars (I use the French brand Le Parfait). Combine ¾ cup of sugar, 1 cup of white wine vinegar (I use homemade), 1 cup of Jurançon sec (a dry white wine made from the Petit and Gros Mensang grapes) or any fruity dry white wine, 1 bay leaf (I use fresh) and a few allspice berries in a saucepan and bring to a simmer for 1 minute. The brine should taste sharp, but adjust and add a little more sugar if your grapes are not particularly sweet. Wait until the brine is completely cool (as hot pickling liquid will cook the grapes, causing them to lose their crunch), then pour it over the grapes. Seal the jars and store in the fridge. Once opened, use within a few days.

Caille braisée aux raisins
BRAISED QUAIL AND GRAPES

The grapes used in this dish are both French AOP varieties: Chasselas and Muscat de Hambourg. They're relatively small grapes compared with common supermarket varieties, and they add beautiful colour and flavour to the dish. If you can't find them, try to source the smallest possible table grape variety you can – too big and they will dominate the dish. This recipe is based on one by David Tanis, one of my greatest culinary gurus.

SERVES 4

8 quail (about 150 g each)

1½ teaspoons minced garlic

1 large sprig lemon thyme, chopped, and 6 large sprigs, left unchopped

2 tablespoons olive oil

1 teaspoon red wine vinegar

1 teaspoon brown sugar

1 bunch (about 200 g) salad onions, roots removed and quartered, keeping the green tops intact (or 200 g small red onions peeled and cut into wedges)

500 g grapes on the stem, cut into approximately 6 small clusters

Rinse the quail and pat them dry. Season each bird inside and out with salt and pepper, then rub with garlic and the chopped lemon thyme. Drizzle the birds with 1 tablespoon olive oil and put in the fridge to marinate overnight. Before cooking, bring the quail back to room temperature.

Preheat your oven to 220 °C. Combine the red wine vinegar, brown sugar and 1 tablespoon olive oil in an ovenproof pan large enough to hold the quail (which will be added to the pan later in the process). Add onions, season with salt and pepper and toss to combine. Roast the onions, stirring occasionally, until caramelised – about 20 minutes. Remove from the pan and set aside on a warm plate.

Place the unchopped sprigs of lemon thyme in the pan and lay the quails on top, breast-side down. Roast for 15 minutes or until puffed and lightly browned, then turn the birds breast-side up and surround with the roasted onions and grape clusters. Return to the oven and roast for 15–20 minutes or until the quail is cooked and golden. Rest for 10–15 minutes in a warm place before serving.

POULTRY REARED GENTLY, FOR QUALITY

Pierre Duplantier raises quail, hens, capons, guineafowl and semi-wild ducklings on his family farm in the foothills of the Béarn. His philosophy of farming, which centres around quality not quantity, sees his birds being delivered to some of France's most elite restaurants: those of Pascal Barbot and Alain Passard, to name just two.

The birds are all free-range until the end of their life, when they're brought into a very quiet, dark barn and fed on a milk-based diet; this results in very tender meat. So important is the wellbeing of the birds to Pierre during this quiet stage that he gently knocks three times before entering the barn in order not to startle them.

Poires et prunes aux noix rôties
dans des feuilles de figues

BAKED PEARS AND PLUMS
ON FIG LEAVES

Arrange halved pears and halved pitted plums cut-side up in a roasting tray lined with freshly picked and washed fig leaves (trim off the leaf stems if they are too long). If you are tempted to omit the fig leaves, don't; they really are key to this dish. The aroma of the roasted leaves will envelop the house in the most heavenly fragrance and impart a subtle coconutty flavour to the pears. Top each half with a walnut and a nob of unsalted butter, sprinkle with cinnamon or freshly grated nutmeg, and roast at 190 °C for 20 minutes. Remove and drizzle a little mountain honey over the fruit, then return to the oven for a further 5 minutes. Cooking time can vary depending on the size and ripeness of the fruit.

Note: I never remove the core and stem from the pear – I just eat around it.

Châtaignes bouillies et grillées au feu
BOILING AND ROASTING CHESTNUTS

I was given this recipe by my friend, Henri, who is the only person to have shared his secret mushroom-foraging spot with me. You can be sure you have a friend in France when someone does this – it's almost unheard of.

When we go mushroom hunting, we always throw some chestnuts into the basket. Henri's method for cooking them is to score the tip of the chestnut (the pointy end) with a cross, and then place the chestnuts in a saucepan with a fresh fig leaf at the bottom and a star anise pod. Fill the saucepan with cold water, bring to the boil, then simmer for 20–35 minutes until cooked (cooking time will depend on the size of the chestnuts – they're generally cooked when the shells begin to curl open a bit). Peel the chestnuts and use in soups and in stuffings for poultry and other meat. Cooked chestnuts can also be used in risottos, braised with meats, candied, made into a sweetened paste for pastry or simply eaten as a snack.

To roast, score the tips as above and toast over hot coals in a chestnut pan. If you can't find one, you can simply drill holes into an old frying pan. The holes allow the chestnuts to toast evenly at a high temperature without burning – but you do need to keep tossing them as they roast.

ANNABELLE AND A VERY SCRUFFY STANLEY ROAST CHESTNUTS GATHERED FROM THE FOREST. ANNABELLE IS WEARING A WOOLEN JUMPER AND SOCKS FROM MAISON IZARD, A LOCAL BÉARNAISE COMPANY WHO PRODUCE ECOLOGICALLY SUSTAINABLE CLOTHING FROM THE FLEECE OF BREBIS EWES, WHOSE MILK IS USED FOR MAKING CHEESE.

La cuisine d'hiver

THE WINTER KITCHEN

ONE CONSTANT IN OUR WINTER KITCHEN is undoubtedly the fanfare that accompanies the Christmas menu; not just the main meal, but the entire festive food extravaganza that, in my opinion, makes Christmas (*Noël*) much more than a one-day event. There's also the rather fraught yet thrilling exercise of constructing a scale model of the entire house and barn in gingerbread, which inevitably sees me collapsed on the sofa afterwards, munching a handful of leftover fence posts and gulping a large glass of Côtes du Rhône.

It's in winter that the AGA stove reigns supreme; a comforting, cosy magnet to warm frozen feet after a frosty morning walk. From any of its four ovens come slow-cooked casseroles, sticky puddings, sweetly spiced cakes, and delicious roast joints of meat. The kitchen is almost permanently enveloped in the scent of cloves, ginger, cinnamon, nutmeg, Armagnac, brown sugar and clementines. It's also in this season that the original kitchen's fireplace in the snug takes on the role of grill. Steaks are cooked here, potatoes baked and chestnuts roasted.

The winter harvest includes

beets – *betteraves*

broccoli – *brocoli*

Brussels sprouts – *choux de Bruxelles*

cabbage – *chou*

carrots – *carottes*

cauliflower – *choufleur*

chard – *bette*

citrus fruits – *agrumes*

endive – *endive*

fennel – *fenouil*

green onions – *oignons verts*

kale – *chou kale*

parsnips – *panais*

pears – *poires*

sweet potatoes – *patates douces*

turnips – *navets*

wild mushrooms – *champignons sauvages*

winter squash – *courge d'hiver*

GARBURE

This typical Béarnaise soup is found on almost every menu in the region. It's a very simple soup that would traditionally have been made using whatever was available in the *potager*, as well as some of the ham and *confit* duck that was stored in the cellar. Regardless of how many people at the table have ordered it, *garbure* is served at country *auberges* in a giant-sized terrine that could feed a small army (I don't know why), from which you serve yourself. Every year in mid-September, the village of Oloron-Sainte-Marie hosts the *garbure* world championships – but, in my humble opinion, I think the best I've tasted comes from an *auberge* called Auberge Claverie, in Audaux, just five minutes from Montfort. Every household in the Béarn has its own version, but this recipe is as authentic as I think you'll find anywhere.

SERVES A SMALL ARMY

250 g dried beans (white beans or black-eyed peas work nicely)

500 g piece of *jambon de Bayonne* on the bone (or 1 ham hock)

9–10 black peppercorns, whole

1 Espelette pepper or ½ teaspoon powdered *piment d'Espelette* (or 1 mild chilli or ½ teaspoon cayenne pepper)

1 onion, studded with 4 cloves

6–7 cm stick celery

1 sprig thyme

1 bay leaf

6 carrots

4 turnips

2 leeks

8 pieces *confit* duck

1 white cabbage

6 potatoes

Soak the beans for 12 hours or overnight. Place the *jambon de Bayonne*, peppercorns, Espelette pepper, clove-studded onion, celery, thyme and bay leaf in a large pot and then cover with 4–5 litres of cold water. Bring to the boil, then reduce to a simmer for 1½ hours. Peel and chop the carrots and turnips into large chunks, and slice the leeks. Fry the pieces of *confit* duck in a pan until golden and then drain on paper towel, reserving all but 4 tablespoons of the duck fat from the pan (this can be stored in the fridge and used at another time to roast potatoes). Add the turnips, carrots and leeks to the pan with the duck fat and sauté for a few minutes. Now place the sautéed vegetables into the pot of stock, along with the drained white beans, and simmer for 2 hours, after which time you can add the sliced white cabbage and simmer for a further 30 minutes. Lastly, add the peeled and roughly chopped potatoes and simmer for 30 minutes more. Before serving, add the *confit* duck and simmer until it is heated through. Taste and adjust the seasoning. Serve with a loaf of rustic country bread (*pain de campagne*).

Note: Traditionally, Béarnaise *garbure* would have been made with *les haricot maïs du Béarn*. This ancient variety of climbing bean is customarily planted beside a corn plant (*maïs*), for support as it twines.

POULE AU POT

Poule au pot is the emblematic dish of the Béarn, thanks to King Henry IV. Born in Pau, he was king of Navarre before he assumed the French throne in 1589. Vowing to bring peace and prosperity after years of war and famine, he declared: 'If God grants me life, I will see that every labouring man in my kingdom shall have his chicken to put in the pot.' Traditionally, this dish would have been cooked in an iron cauldron over the fire. It's not complicated to make, but it takes time – and, unfortunately, *time* has become confused with *complicated*. You can follow this recipe closely, or use what you've got: all the ingredients for *poule au pot* would typically be found in a Béarnaise garden. This includes the chicken, usually a Cou-Nu (one of the least attractive chickens I've ever seen, because it has no neck feathers), a breed renowned for its meat. If you are using your own selection of vegetables, remember that their cooking times will vary depending on size and type, so add them to the broth progressively. I serve this dish with a little bowl of *sauce ravigote*. This sauce is not traditionally served with *poule au pot* in the Béarn (in fact, it's more usually served with veal's head, *tête de veau*), but in my humble opinion it gives the finished dish a lovely brightness.

SERVES 6

STUFFING INGREDIENTS

chicken liver and giblets, finely chopped

300 g veal or pork mince

2 slices white bread

100 ml milk

1 egg, lightly beaten

3 garlic cloves, finely chopped

2 tablespoons chopped parsley

1 teaspoon chopped lemon thyme

¼ teaspoon freshly grated nutmeg

2 finely chopped shallots (French *échalotes*)

Prepare the stuffing as follows. In a medium-sized bowl, combine the chopped chicken liver and giblets with the mince. In another bowl, place the bread in the milk to soften, mash with a fork and then combine with the beaten egg. Combine the meat and bread mixture with the remaining stuffing ingredients and season with salt and pepper. Stuff the chicken with this mixture and secure it by trussing the legs with string.

Prepare a bouquet garni with the green parts of the leeks, the bay leaves and the parsley by tying them together with string or enclosing them in a muslin pouch. Pour 3 litres of water into a large casserole dish. Add the coarse salt, onion, cloves, garlic, the bouquet garni and the chicken. Cover and cook in the broth for 1½ hours, skimming occasionally.

While the chicken is cooking, prepare the vegetables. Cut the cabbage into six equal portions and blanch in a pot of boiling water for 1–2 minutes (this makes the cabbage much more digestible). Drain, then add to the pot with the remaining vegetables, seasoning with salt and pepper to taste. Simmer for another 30 minutes (or less if you are using smaller vegetables such as baby turnips).

FOR THE POT

1.3 kg free-range organic chicken, trimmed of excess fat (reserve liver and giblets for the stuffing)

4 small leeks, trimmed, cleaned and cut into short lengths

1–2 bay leaves

3–4 sprigs parsley

3 tablespoons coarse salt

2 onions, peeled and quartered

6 cloves

1 small head of garlic, cut in half horizontally

¼ cabbage

2–3 carrots, peeled and cut into 4 cm pieces

400 g potatoes, peeled and halved if large

3 celery sticks, cut into short lengths

2 turnips, peeled and quartered

1 sprig lemon thyme, for garnish

SAUCE RAVIGOTE

1 tablespoon Dijon mustard

2 tablespoons white wine vinegar

½ cup sunflower oil

3–4 cornichons, finely chopped

1 tablespoon chopped capers

2 shallots (French *échalotes*), finely chopped

Finely chopped parsley, chervil and tarragon (enough for 1 tablespoon)

Remove the cooked chicken from the broth (if you have a food thermometer, the internal temperature of the thigh should be 70°C). Don't discard the stock from the pot, it makes a delicious soup. Dice any leftover vegetables and chicken, add them to the broth and refrigerate for the next day. It's excellent with homemade soda bread and lashings of French butter!

Transfer to a carving board, allow to rest for at least 10 minutes, then remove the string and turn the chicken upside down. Using poultry scissors, cut along either side of the backbone to remove it. Prise the chicken open and remove the stuffing in one piece. Quarter the chicken and slice the stuffing. Put the chicken in the centre of a heated platter. Arrange the stuffing in overlapping slices around the chicken. Spoon a few tablespoons of the hot stock over the chicken to moisten. Garnish with thyme.

SAUCE RAVIGOTE

Combine the mustard and white wine vinegar in a bowl. Season with salt and freshly ground pepper. Begin whisking, slowly drizzling in the oil and whisking continuously as you incorporate the oil as you would for a vinaigrette. Add cornichons, capers, shallots and herbs. Mix to combine and adjust seasoning.

BÉARNAISE SAUCE

This sauce is actually not Béarnaise. It was created by Jean-Louis Françoise-Collinet some time around the 1830s and named in honour of the restaurant for which it was first made, Le Pavillon Henri IV, near Paris – a former residence of King Henry IV.

Confit de canard
CONFIT DUCK
(FOR LAZY DAYS)

Confit de canard can be made with almost any part of the bird – legs, thigh meat, heart, wing tips and gizzards all work. The fresh meat is simply seasoned with salt and pepper and perhaps a bay leaf or sprig of thyme, left for two days in the fridge, then slowly cooked in a bath of duck fat until meltingly tender. If you're doing your own confit, four legs will take around 3 hours in a 110°C oven, but you'll want to season them 6–12 hours in advance.

Once cooked, the duck pieces are removed, placed in a container and stored in a thick layer of the duck fat until needed. Traditionally, they were stored in stoneware confit crocks that were covered with cloth and tied with string. These days, you generally buy confit duck in a tin. Because the tinned meat is already cooked, it's a great meal to have on hand for lazy days when you don't want much fuss – the French cook's version of fast food. My favourite way to serve confit duck legs as a family meal begins with peeling 6–8 medium potatoes. Simply remove the confit duck legs from the thick layer of duck fat in the tin, scrape as much fat as you can from the legs and then place 3 or 4 tablespoons of the fat in the baking tray that you will use to roast the potatoes. Spoon the remaining duck fat into a glass storage jar (I use hinged, lidded Le Parfait jars with a rubber seal) and keep in the fridge for later use. Melt the duck fat in the tray in a hot oven, then toss the peeled potatoes in the fat and roast until crispy. When they're almost done, lay the duck legs flat on a baking tray skin-side up and bake in a moderate oven until they are hot. I serve this dish with steamed green beans.

THE SWEET LITTLE BRACKEN ROOVED KINTOA PIG HOUSES AT PIERRE OTEIZA'S FARM IN LES ALDUDES VALLEY.

234

THE *TUE-COCHON*

Here in the Béarn, January is the time of the *tue-cochon*: farm-reared pigs are slaughtered, and families gather together to butcher and preserve the meat. As long as the pig has been raised on a family farm and is intended for personal consumption, this tradition is permitted by French law to be carried out on the premises. It's a three-day process, possibly best described as a great big party (though not for the pig), starting with the killing on the first day and concluding with the making of sausage, *saucisson* (similar to salami), *rillettes de porc* and pâtés. Every part of the pig is used, including the blood. In raising that pig, every bit of the previous season's household vegetable and fruit waste is fed to the animal. Montfort holds a village competition to see who can raise the fattest, with all sorts of fiercely guarded secrets for achieving the porkiest pig.

THE SPRING KITCHEN

THE RETURN OF LONGER DAYS AND THE joy of spring is something I long for in the depths of winter (despite being an avid downhill skier). Come spring, the garden requires my attention. Seedlings need to be planted out as the soil warms. There are weeds to pluck, and flowers to gather and arrange into blousy bouquets throughout the house. I also spend hours under the magnolia tree, picking tiny wild violets to decorate cakes while inhaling their heavenly sweet scent. The nettles are at their most tender at this time of year, often featuring in risottos and soups. It's also time for harvesting garlic and plaiting it into trusses to dry. Spring lamb is on the menus of local *auberges*, and by late May shepherds are preparing to return to their mountain huts for the summer. Hiking is again on the agenda, and as winter snows melt, the Pyrénées erupt into a carpet of wildflowers. The salmon and trout are jumping, and life once more becomes a glorious celebration of colour, birdsong and renewed energy.

The spring harvest includes

apricots – *abricots*

artichokes – *artichauts*

asparagus – *asperges*

bear's garlic – *ail des ours*

beets – *betteraves*

bitter greens – *laitues amères*

broad beans – *haricots de fava*

carrots – *carottes*

peas – *pois*

potatoes – *pommes de terre*

radishes – *radis*

rhubarb – *rhubarbe*

snow peas – *pois mange-tout*

spinach – *épinard*

strawberries – *fraises*

zucchini – *courgettes*

MY VINAIGRETTE MADE IN THE BOWL

It might sound strange, but the secret to a good vinaigrette starts with a good salad bowl. It has to be the right size for the amount of salad you need to prepare, but most importantly it needs to be shallow and round. Unless I'm making salad for a big crowd, I use my most coveted salad bowl, one made by local potters Madame and Monsieur Charpentier, of Poterie Parabis. The bowl (which is 30 centimetres wide and 5 centimetres deep) is glazed in their signature blues and browns, and its smooth, shiny finish is absolutely perfect for mixing the vinaigrette directly in the bowl – which, in my opinion, is exactly where a French vinaigrette should be made. The recipe that follows is here simply to guide you. Vinaigrette in France is generally made *au pif*, 'by the nose', or as we say in English, by eye. I never measure; I judge the quantity I need *au pif*, adding the ingredients straight into the bowl. But to begin with, these ratios will be a good guide for a green salad to serve 6 people (based on roughly 1 lettuce – anything but iceberg).

ENOUGH TO DRESS A LARGE GREEN SALAD

½ garlic clove (optional)

1 tablespoon chopped shallot (French *échalote*)

2 tablespoons good-quality red wine vinegar or sherry vinegar (these vinegars reflect my preference, but you can also use white wine vinegar, which is more typical)

½–1 teaspoon French mustard, according to taste (by French mustard, I *mean* French – I use either Maille Moutarde Fine de Dijon or Amora Moutarde de Dijon)

6 tablespoons mildly flavoured olive oil or organic sunflower oil

Rub the bowl with the cut end of the garlic clove (optional). Add the chopped shallot, a pinch of salt and the red wine vinegar, and let the mixture rest for a few minutes for the flavours to infuse. Whisk in the mustard until the mixture is smooth. Follow this by whisking in the mildly flavoured olive oil or sunflower oil (which is even milder again and, if it's good quality, slightly nutty in flavour) until it is fully incorporated. Taste and adjust the seasoning. Add the washed salad leaves and use your hands to toss them in the vinaigrette until they're coated. Serve immediately.

Variations: For a creamy dressing, you can whisk in 1 teaspoon of crème fraîche at the end of the process, before you add the salad leaves. Lots of French people I know add a few drops of Maggi liquid seasoning to their vinaigrettes; it adds, they tell me, a certain *je ne sais quoi*.

ESTO PESTO

Take your cues from the landscape around you. This simple sauce was first made by our dear friend Esther (who also happens to be the namesake for one of our goats) after she collected some of the nettles and wild mint that grow in our back field, on her way home from feeding our chickens. The addition of sunflower kernels was inspired by the crops that surround our house in summer. Foraged nettles can also be used to make a soup, *soupe d'orties*. Basque shepherds use nettle leaves to strain sheep's milk when they graze and milk their flocks in the Pyrénées during the summer.

To make this sauce you will need 2–3 good handfuls of freshly picked nettle leaves – the tender leaves at the top of the plant are best. Pick the nettles wearing rubber gloves, then pour boiling water over the leaves to neutralise the sting caused by the tiny hairs on the plant. Toast 3–4 tablespoons of sunflower seeds in a small pan over the stove. Put the nettles, a handful of wild apple mint or regular mint, salt, pepper, a little grated garlic and the toasted sunflower kernels into a food processor. Whiz the nettle mixture, adding olive oil until you have a creamy consistency, then taste and adjust the seasonings to suit your palate. If you want a sharper flavour – for example, to spoon over grilled meats – simply add a little red wine vinegar and chopped capers to taste; this will thin the mixture into more of a sauce.

Conserve d'ail au vinaigre parfumé aux herbes du jardin
PICKLED GARLIC WITH GARDEN HERBS

This recipe for quick pickled garlic is very easy to prepare and will last 3–4 months in the fridge. Combine 6 teaspoons of salt and 2½ cups of white wine vinegar, bring to the boil and then simmer for 5–10 minutes. Into two sterilised jars (I usually use a 324 millilitre Le Parfait jam jar or a recycled jar of similar size), pack enough peeled garlic to come just up to the top of the shoulder of the jar. To this, add a bay leaf, a scattering of whole red peppercorns and a sprig each of rosemary and lemon thyme. If you grow your own lavender, you can add just a few flowers; these have a fresh flavour similar to rosemary. Pour the hot pickling liquid over the garlic and seal the jars immediately. Leave in the refrigerator for 2–3 weeks before using – to allow the flavours to develop.

The pickled cloves are bright and punchy in flavour. I often use them in a relish that is great with grilled mackerel, chicken or steak, but it honestly seems to work with almost anything. Simply soak a few tablespoons of currants in sherry vinegar until plump, before combining with chopped cornichons, finely chopped pickled garlic, olive oil and some finely diced red onion.

OVERLEAF: HUBERT MILKING HIS EWES.
A NEWBORN LIES IN THE STRAW WAITING FOR ITS MOTHER.

SHEEP'S MILK FROM A LOCAL SHEPHERD

One of the great pleasures of living so close to a shepherd is being able to pop down the road and bring home a jug of milk so fresh that it's warm, which I often use to make a sheep's-milk curd, *caillé de brebis*. Hubert Wurth, our local shepherd, milks every one of his 200 ewes by hand every day. It's incredibly peaceful stroking a newborn lamb in his barn and watching the ewes being hand-milked as they stand knee-deep in soft, fresh straw.

When the milking is finished, they happily trot off into another pen for a dinner of fresh hay. It's all done in complete silence, with just the peaceful background rustling of straw, slow contented munching and the rhythmic percussion of milk landing in the bucket. The only time I don't make *caillé* with milk from Hubert's ewes is in the summer, when he and his *troupeau* of sheep are in the mountains.

Caillé de brebis

There is no good translation for this quintessentially French dessert of lightly set ewe's curd. Ewe's milk has significantly higher levels of milk solids (fat and protein) than other milks and has roughly double the fat content of cow or goat milk. However, the average ewe produces less than a gallon (3.75 litres) of milk a day, whereas a cow can produce 6–8 gallons (23–30 litres) a day. If you can't source ewe's milk (note that milk is legally required to be sold in pasteurised form in many countries outside of France, including the UK and Australia), use full fat organic cow's milk with a dash of extra cream. I buy my rennet from the pharmacy and store it in the fridge; outside of small French villages, it can usually be found in specialty food stores or large health food stores.

Bring 1 litre of ewe's milk and 1 split vanilla bean to a slight boil in a saucepan. Add 1 tablespoon of sugar and whisk to combine. Remove from the heat and allow to cool down to 37°C (measure this with a food thermometer). If you are preparing individual servings in a jar with a 250 millilitre capacity, place 1–2 drops of rennet in the base of each jar; anything smaller than this requires only 1 drop of rennet. (I often use squat, round, Spanish wine glasses or recycled French glass yoghurt pots with a capacity of 125 millilitres, so one drop for these.) Scrape out the seeds from the vanilla pod and whisk again. Pour the 37°C milk into each glass, then cover with a towel and place in the fridge to set (there's no need to mix). Serve with freshly shelled new-season walnuts and slightly warmed mountain wildflower honey. Alternatively, it's very good with a spoonful of Basque Itxassou cherry jam; the Basques make this delicious jam from the Peloa, Xapata and Beltxa Basque heirloom cherry varieties. Shepherds typically pour a shot of espresso over *caillé de brebis*, along with some sugar, and eat it for breakfast.

Confiture de pétales de rose et rhubarbe
ROSE PETAL AND RHUBARB JAM

This jam, inspired by the fabulous Diana Henry, is one I make in spring, when the first of my roses are in flower and the new season's rhubarb is just emerging from its winter slumber. I always have loads of jam jars on hand, usually 324 millilitre Le Parfait *pots à confiture*. I use a large traditional copper jam pan; a gift from an old friend when I lived in Moscow. As with all jams, it's important to let the fruit macerate with the sugar overnight, or for at least 12 hours in advance of cooking. If you're using a copper jam pan, this maceration process is also essential in order to avoid the fruit acids coming into direct contact with the copper. This jam is beautiful with a slice of toasted brioche (or on scones with lashings of whipped cream).

MAKES 3 KG

2 kg rhubarb (roughly 2 bunches), cut into 1¼-cm pieces

5 cups (1.1 kg) jam sugar (or 5 cups caster sugar with 14 g pectin added)

2 Granny Smith apples, finely chopped

1 lemon, juiced

6 cardamom pods, bruised

2 cups rose petals, bases trimmed

1 teaspoon rose water (if you don't have any rose petals, you can double the amount of rose water)

Place the chopped rhubarb, sugar and apples in a large bowl and mix well. Leave to macerate overnight or for at least 12 hours (cover with a clean tea towel).

Pour the fruit into a copper jam pan, or a heavy-bottomed Dutch oven, and bring it slowly to the boil, skimming off any scum that rises to the surface. Add the lemon juice and cardamom and continue boiling until the mixture reaches 105 °C on a sugar thermometer, or until a small amount wrinkles when pushed on a cold plate (place the plate in the freezer in advance). This stage is usually reached after 15–20 minutes of boiling. Allow the jam to sit for 5–10 minutes, then stir in the rose petals and rose water. Ladle into sterilised jam jars.

SOURCING GUIDE

Although many of the companies listed here do not have region-specific websites, do not be deterred – almost all of them either offer international delivery or are available via local stockists, which are listed on their websites.

PAINT

Please note, the paint colours as you see them on the page will differ slightly from the true paint colour once it is applied. This is due both to the different compositions of CMYK inks and paint and the fact that each surface material holds colour differently. Please use the colour codes provided to refer to the colour swatches given on the NCS website or on the Colourpin mobile app, and order sample pots to test whether the paint colours match your expectations.

Argile
argile-peinture.com

Autentico
autentico-paint.co.uk
autentico-paint.fr
autentico-paint.com

Bauwerk
bauwerkcolour.com

Benjamin Moore Paints
benjaminmoore.com

Farrow & Ball (also offers wallpaper)
farrow-ball.com

Libéron
liberon.fr
liberon.co.uk
liberon.com.au

The Little Green Paint Company Ltd (also offers wallpaper)
littlegreene.com

Ressource (also offers wallpaper)
ressource-peintures.com
ressource-decoration.com

TEXTILES

Tissues d'Helene (tissusdhelene.co.uk) and Sanderson Design Group (sandersondesign.group) are wonderful UK-based resources for many of the following companies, as well as Anstey, Anthology, Clarke & Clarke, Harlequin, Morris & Co., Scion, Standfast & Barracks and Zoffany.

Anna Spiro Textiles
annaspirotextiles.com.au

Bouchara (well-priced fabric by the metre and French homewares)
bouchara.com

Caï Fahrel
caifahrel.com

The Cloth Shop (linen and Indian block print fabrics – UK and Europe only)
theclothshop.net

Décors Barbares
decorsbarbares.com

Elliott Clarke
elliottclarke.com.au

Langton Textiles
langtontextiles.co.uk

Lebenskleidung (denim, chambray and canvas by the metre)
lebenskleidung.com

Lisa Fine Textiles
lisafinetextiles.com

Nicole Fabre Designs
nicolefabredesigns.com

Pigott's Store
pigottsstore.com.au

Pukka Print (also offers wallpaper)
pukkaprintlinen.com

Schuyler Samperton Textiles
schuylersampertontextiles.com

Sister Parish Design (also offers wallpaper)
sisterparishdesign.com

Titley and Marr
titleyandmarr.co.uk

Passementerie

Declercq
declercqpassementiers.fr

Fringe Market
fringemarket.com

Houlès
houles.com

Passementerie Verrier
passementerie-verrier.com

WALLPAPER

Adelphi Paper Hangings
adelphipaperhangings.com

Anaglypta (embossed wallpapers)
anaglypta.co.uk

Antoinette Poisson
antoinettepoisson.com

Borastapeter
borastapeter.com

de Gournay (handpainted wallpapers)
degournay.com

Dufour Wallpapers
dufourwallpapers.com

Gracie (handpainted wallpapers)
graciestudio.com

Pierre Frey
pierrefrey.com

Sandberg
sandbergwallpaper.com

Zuber (also offers textiles)
zuber.fr

HOMEWARE

Local artisans, craft fairs, flea markets, auction houses and vintage and antique shops are wonderful places to hunt for those finishing details. However, online marketplaces like Selency (selency.co.uk) Etsy (etsy.com) and eBay (ebay.com) will almost always have something to offer.

Atelier Vime
ateliervime.com

Cushion Warehouse (custom feather cushions)
cushionwarehouse.co.uk

Jielde Lights (French-made industrial lamps)
jielde.com

Leonard Joel (auction house)
leonardjoel.com.au

Nyary ES (antiques)
nyary.com.au

Olde Brick Lighting (lights, seen in the barn bedrooms)
oldebricklighting.com

Parna (textiles)
parna.co.uk

Parterre (antiques)
parterre.com.au

Suzie Anderson Home
suzieandersonhome.com

Vickers & Hoad (auction house)
vickhoad.com

KITCHEN AND DINING

For a full fit-out, I can't speak highly enough of Handmade Kitchens Direct (handmadekitchens-direct.co.uk), who did all of the main kitchen joinery in the barn. And for stoves, it's hard to beat the classics: Lacanche (lacanche.fr) and Lacornue (lacornue.com).

Cookware

Manufacture de Digoin (mixing bowls, confit pots and vinegar pots)
manufacturededigoin.com

Mauviel (copper pots)
mauviel.com

Opinel (kitchen and outdoor knives)
opinel.com

Pallares Solsona (kitchen knives)
pallaressolsona.com

Staub (cast-iron pots)
staub-online.com

Tableware

Gien (crockery)
gien.com

Jean Dubost (kitchen knives and tableware)
jeandubost.fr

Laguiole (kitchen knives and tableware)
laguiole-attitude.com

La Rochere (glassware)
larochere.com

Pillivuyt (crockery)
pillivuyt.fr

ACKNOWLEDGEMENTS

To the sensational team at Thames & Hudson, my heartfelt thanks. Kirsten Abbott, thank you for commissioning this book and for your enduring faith in me. I am forever grateful. And thank you Sam Palfreyman, my editor, for your immense patience and excellent pair of eagle eyes, you are a true gem.

To my book designer, Daniel New, your talent is simply breathtaking. I'm so honoured that *How to French Country* is among the many beautiful books that bear your irrefutable flair.

To the gorgeous Diana Hill, thank you for whipping my very flabby manuscript into the sleek and trim version that exists today. Working with you was a joy.

To my talented illustrator, Valérie Micheaux (otherwise known in our household as Valérie Micheaux-Angelo), you are a true master! Thank you for creating such a beautiful regional map.

Thanks too to the lovely Grace Campbell for recipe testing, and to Emma Vicassiau for assisting me with communications and for being such a beautiful friend.

To my literary agent, Charlie Brotherstone, Brotherstone Creative Management; *merci mille fois.*

To my IEFE professors at the Université de Pau et des Pays de l'Adour (UPPA): thank you for your immense generosity, your long-suffering patience, and for igniting my passion for the Béarn and French language and culture. And to Jean-Jacques Casteret, Professor Patricia Heiniger-Casteret and Professor Laurent Dissard in particular, thank you for your wonderful leads and insights into Béarnaise culture and your constant support and enthusiasm.

To Jacques Pedehontaa, mayor of Làas, and Clarisse Haigneré of Tourism 64, thank you both for fielding my many questions and for the regional passion you provided along the way.

To Clément Guillemot and Flora Le Pape of Choko Ona, Espelette; thank you for your support and friendship. I'm blessed to have met you both.

To the Mayor of Montfort, and the people of Montfort, *merci bien* for making me so welcome in your community.

To all the artisans who have worked with me for the past five years – Dédé Chabalgoity, Jean-Marc Idiart, Patrice Cabale, Lionel Dumont, Claude Sarhy, Alex De Souza, Franck Ayerdi, Jean Oyenhart and Bertrand Souviron. Thank you for being the best team of artisans I could have wished for.

To all the volunteers from Workaway, who have helped us build goat and chicken houses, renovate the garden, exchanged recipes, shared food at our table and enriched our lives, *bisous*.

To my darling husband, Jason Silm, and our treasured children, Hugo, Annabelle and Toby. Thank you for being the wheels that kept this train on the tracks. You are my everything.

To my parents, my friends and my entire extended family, thank you for your unfailing support, I love you.

And finally, to all the artisans and suppliers I have worked with: thank you for making this world more beautiful with your talent and creativity.

All wallpaper designs, textile designs and paint colour names referred to in this book are the registered trademarks of their associated companies. NCS – Natural Colour System®© property of and used on licence from NCS Colour AB, Stockholm 2018. References to NCS®© in this publication are used with permission from the NCS Colour AB.

First published in Australia in 2021
by Thames & Hudson Australia Pty Ltd
11 Central Boulevard, Portside Business Park
Port Melbourne, Victoria 3207
ABN: 72 004 751 964

First published in the United Kingdom in 2022
by Thames & Hudson Ltd
181a High Holborn
London WC1V 7QX

First published in the United States of America in 2022
by Thames & Hudson Inc.
500 Fifth Avenue
New York, New York 10110

How to French Country © Thames & Hudson Australia 2021

Text and Illustrations © Sara Silm 2021

Copyright in all text and images is held by the author or their representatives, unless otherwise stated.

24 23 22   5 4 3 2

The moral right of the author has been asserted.

All rights reserved. No part of this publication may be reproduced or transmitted in any form or by any means, electronic or mechanical, including photocopy, recording or any other information storage or retrieval system, without prior permission in writing from the publisher.

Any copy of this book issued by the publisher is sold subject to the condition that it shall not by way of trade or otherwise be lent, resold, hired out or otherwise circulated without the publisher's prior consent in any form or binding or cover other than that in which it is published and without a similar condition including these words being imposed on a subsequent purchaser.

Thames & Hudson Australia wishes to acknowledge that Aboriginal and Torres Strait Islander people are the first storytellers of this nation and the traditional custodians of the land on which we live and work. We acknowledge their continuing culture and pay respect to Elders past, present and future.

ISBN 978-1-760-76098-4 (hardback)
ISBN 978-1-760-76245-2 (U.S. edition)

A catalogue record for this book is available from the National Library of Australia

British Library Cataloguing-in-Publication Data
A catalogue record for this book is available from the British Library

Library of Congress Control Number 2021940812

Every effort has been made to trace accurate ownership of copyrighted text and visual materials used in this book. Errors or omissions will be corrected in subsequent editions, provided notification is sent to the publisher.

Map illustration for endpapers by Valérie Micheaux © Sara Silm 2021

Design: Daniel New
Editing: Diana Hill

Printed and bound in China by 1010 Printing International Limited.

Be the first to know about our new releases, exclusive content and author events by visiting
thamesandhudson.com.au
thamesandhudson.com
thamesandhudsonusa.com

FSC® is dedicated to the promotion of responsible forest management worldwide. This book is made of material from FSC®-certified forests and other controlled sources.